STREET FARM

1799

Mrs Collins
Common
39
Great Highgate
3.0.7
38
Little Highgate
1.3.27
16
Little Coombs
3.0.4
Mr Wm Gunner
Windmill Plot
36
0.2.18
37
Highgate Six Acres
5.2.39
Mr Wm Gunner
31
Barfield
1.2.38
21
Long Close
3.2.10
31
Alms Acre
1.0.16
32
Upper and Lower Windmill Field
6.2.10
33
Upper and Lower Hook Lane
3.3.20
Long Field
3.2.15
Mr Allen Iunson
To Frimley
29
Hop Garden
1.2.36
22
Lower Wood
6.2.5
28
Upper Wood Field
4.1.18
30
Ladies Plat
1.2.24
27
Croft
0.2.2
Hook Lane
19
3.1.12
25
Coopers Close
0.3.12
20
Coopers Plat
1.1.16
1
Potatoe Field
1.1.39
8
Reeds Close
2.1.37
5
Barn Field
2.1.6
2
Two Acre Plat
2.0.22
13
Wool Mead
3.3.12
12
Priors Plats
4.0.6
Waste
4
Tanners Mead
2.1.14
Mr Allen Iunson
11
Little Priors
1.2.30
10
Priors Meadow
5.0.36
9
Reeds Meadow
4.3.34
3
Hatch Mead
2.1.1
of Surrey

Farnborough

A PICTORIAL HISTORY

One Hundred Years under the Flight Path

Aerial view of central Farnborough in the early 1960s.

Farnborough

A PICTORIAL HISTORY

One Hundred Years under the Flight Path

Jo Gosney

Phillimore

2005

Published by
PHILLIMORE & CO. LTD
Shopwyke Manor Barn, Chichester, West Sussex, England
www.phillimore.co.uk

ISBN 1 86077 347 8

Printed and bound in Great Britain by
CAMBRIDGE PRINTING

List of Illustrations

Acknowledgements

The author wishes to acknowledge the following for permission to reproduce illustrations:

Aerofilms & St Peter's Junior School, 1; Aldershot & District Bus Interest Group, 97; The late Mr B. Allum, 144, 148; Dr J. Attenborough, 5; Mrs J. Bailey, 94; Mr A.A. Cook MM, 63; Mr L. Cook, 36, 121; Mr H. Davies, 153; Col M. A. Demetriadi, 125, 126; Mrs M. Dodd, 13, 123; Mrs A. Dowrick, 136; The Drachen Foundation, 98; F.A.S.T. Archives, 119, 122; Mr J. Gaines, 16, 93, 95, 96, 151, 169, 170, 171, 172; Mr W.E. Gosney, 159; Mr P. Grantham, 85, 86, 87; Mr J. Grenham, 53, 54, 55, 56, 59, 61, 62, 91, 92; Mrs E. Hack, 41; Mrs K. Hall, 2; Mrs J. Hicks, 83, 114; Mr P. Hicks, 138, 152; Mrs P. Hill, 71; Mrs E. Hughes, 99; Mr J. Knight, 37, 89; Mr D. Lelliott, 150; Mr L.A. Loveday, 161; Miss M. Lowrey, 18, 20, 21, 22; Mr A. Lunn, 44; Mrs M. Morgan, 149; Mr J. Oliver, 40, 84; Mrs A. Rayne, 131, 132, 133; Mrs B. Stickland, 146; Mr J. Thripp, 154, 155; Mr P. Vickery, 6, 7, 35, 51, 75, 80, 128, 129, 130; Mrs P. Wilson, 156, 157, 158; Mrs B. Woolger, 14; Mr A.P. Worgan, 38, 39, 135, 147; Mr R. Yeoman, 127, 142, 162; 70, Handbill © Royal Mail Group plc. Reproduced by kind permission of Royal Mail. All Rights Reserved.

Thanks are also due to the staff at Aldershot Military Museum, Farnborough Library, Rushmoor Borough Council and the volunteers at the Farnborough Air Sciences Trust Museum for their assistance with research; and again I am indebted to Jim Gaines for his photographic help and my ever supportive husband Michael for his patience whilst I have been writing this book.

Introduction

The year 2005 marks the centenary of the move of the Balloon Factory from Aldershot to Farnborough. This event was to mould the shape of the future development and prosperity of what was then a small town on the edge of the Home of the British Army.

The town leaders of the day noted that that there had been considerable clearance of the trees next to the common behind the *Swan Inn* and that a new structure was being erected on Government land. It was also noted that, although Farnborough Road was being churned up by construction vehicles, it was not considered that any undue increase in traffic was likely to be generated in the foreseeable future. Thus was the inauspicious birth of an age of flying and aeronautical research for which Farnborough has become famous.

Readers of my earlier book, *Farnborough Past*, will know that the inhabitants of Farnborough can look to the records of over a thousand years to find their historical roots. This new book endeavours to enhance that record by illustrating the social history of the town as recorded by the camera during the past one hundred years. There will also be references to earlier events because, in order to appreciate the present, it is important to have an understanding of the past. The majority of photographs have come from private collections whose owners have been happy to share their treasures and the stories that go with them. Where postcards have been used, the messages they contain often provide an interesting insight into the activities of the day and they also help to date events with a degree of accuracy. With so much information being stored on computers in this digital age, the photographic record is vital so that it is accessible to all in a tangible and readable way.

The earliest part of the town is centred today in an area called Farnborough Street, where there are some old cottages dating back to the 18th century. Situated on the edge of the Blackwater River, the early village was recorded in Domesday Book as 'Ferne Berga' meaning 'Hill of Ferns'. Known to have been in existence during Anglo-Saxon times, it was willed as part of the hundred of Crondall to Ethelm, the nephew of King Alfred. Having always been rather isolated in the north-eastern corner of the county, the parish developed more or less unaffected by outside influences until the coming of the railway in the mid-19th century. Prior to that time, the main occupation was farming along with a small pottery industry dating back to the mid-14th century.

The parish church, with its 14th-century wall paintings, 15th-century porch and 17th-century tower, is sited on a hill on the outskirts of the old village, where it is thought there was an earlier place of Anglo-Saxon worship. The manor house nearby was the seat of the Earls of Anglesey for many years and is believed to have been rebuilt in the late 17th century to a design by Sir Christopher Wren. This important building is now home to St Peter's Junior School. Over the years until the beginning of the 20th century, portions of the manorial lands were sold off piecemeal and it is not difficult even today to identify such areas.

The middle of the 18th century saw a large acreage sold in the north of the parish which created the Farnborough Hill Estate, originally named Windmill Hill, the windmill being situated on the eastern side. An earlier house was demolished in the early 19th century and rebuilt by James Ludovic Grant. Subsequently owned by a Mrs Foreman, it was then bought and demolished by Thomas Longman, the publisher, who erected the present building, now known as Farnborough Hill, in 1860. An imposing, ornate mansion, in a prominent position, it was purchased in 1880 by the Empress Eugenie, the widow of the exiled Emperor Napoleon III of France. The imperial family had fled France and settled in Chislehurst, Kent. When the Emperor died the Empress wanted to build a mausoleum for his remains but was unable to purchase sufficient land at Chislehurst. Eventually, through her friendship with Queen Victoria, she found Farnborough Hill, only 15 miles distant from Windsor, where she was able to purchase sufficient land nearby for the mausoleum. St Michael's was duly built along with a monastery to accommodate the Order of Premonstratensian monks who came over from France to protect the mausoleum beneath the abbey. The remains of the Empress and her son, Prince Louis Napoleon, are also buried there.

After the death of the Empress in 1920, the family retained the house until it was sold in 1926 to become a convent school. Much of the remainder of the estate was sold for building plots which today form the Empress Estate on the west of Farnborough Hill, and on Highgate Lane to the south.

The arrival of the railway in 1838, followed by the government's decision in 1853 to establish the Army in nearby Aldershot, brought about further development.

The main line from London, part of the London and South Western Railway, reached Farnborough in 1838. A small station was constructed which was rapidly enlarged when the line opened up to the south coast and Queen Victoria began to use it on a regular basis. She would often drive by horse and carriage from Windsor to join the train on her journey to Osborne House on the Isle of Wight. Her reviews of the troops in Aldershot also brought her through Farnborough as there was no main-line station in Aldershot until 1870. Thus it was that a small rural village was blessed with a very imposing railway station containing purpose-built royal waiting rooms.

Within ten years another railway line was laid through the old part of the village to link the north-west coast to the channel ports. This belonged to the South Eastern & Chatham Railway but the station was also given the same name of Farnborough. This often caused great confusion to troops embarking for overseas duty, particularly at the time of the Crimean War. On occasions, large numbers of soldiers ended up marching to the wrong station, so eventually the South Eastern station was renamed Farnborough North.

The army immediately recognised the usefulness of the railway for the transportation of horse, troops and guns and both stations extended platforms and sidings specifically for military use.

Although the original village centre was in Farnborough Street, the main-line railway station was about a mile away near Farnborough Road. Many businesses sprang up in the immediate vicinity, then gradually moved and more opened up along the road towards Aldershot and Cove.

The Basingstoke Canal was constructed in 1798 just to the south of the parish boundary. As a waterway it was of little economic benefit to Farnborough although it provided a welcome pleasure facility. For a few years it was used for transporting pottery but it proved more useful for the delivery of materials for the construction of the army camp. The military camp was built as North Camp and South Camp and was divided by the canal. The North Camp lay within the parish of Farnborough and its establishment had a profound effect on the fortunes of the villagers. Many of them found work in the construction of the camp and almost overnight shops and businesses were set up along its northern edge to serve the needs of the soldiers. This, in turn, required houses for people to live in and subsequently more shops to serve the largely expanded civilian population.

This dramatic increase in the population also put pressure on the small parish church and the rector. The tiny churchyard soon became overcrowded, necessitating the building of a new cemetery in Victoria Road as well as the erection of the new church of St Mark in the south of the parish.

Over the next 100 years, the shopping facilities of North Camp expanded, attracting many big stores including Thomas White, Home & Colonial, Woolworths, International Stores, Mence Smith, Co-op, Timothy White's, Boot's the Chemist, and many more. Numerous barbershops, hairdressers, bakers, teashops, tailors and photographers quickly established themselves; Lynchford Road alone had seven boot-and-shoe shops. They, along with furniture stores and funeral directors, auctioneers and estate agents, cinemas and public houses, all drew trade from the camp and the surrounding villages of Frimley, Mytchett, Ash, Ash Vale, Cove and Hawley.

The army camp, with its regimented lines of tents and huts, became home to thousands of soldiers, but the officers needed more comfortable housing. It was not surprising, therefore, that property developers acted swiftly to buy more land from the lord of the manor to build large houses in South Farnborough, on the edge of the camp. This, of course, provided more employment for villagers who were able to enter into service in the big houses.

The concentration of commerce and development in the southern part of the town in the late 19th century made it the obvious choice for the seat of local government. Changes in local government brought about the formation of the Farnborough Urban District Council in 1895 and the Town Hall was built in Alexandra Road the following year. An attractive, well designed building, its large public hall and committee rooms served the town well for more than 80 years. In 1974, further re-organisation of local government brought about amalgamation with nearby Aldershot to form Rushmoor Borough Council. New Council Offices were then constructed towards the centre of Farnborough but the old Town Hall remains as private offices.

Here, I feel, one further aspect of local government needs a mention. In 1932, the administrative boundaries of the town expanded to encompass the village of Cove. The history of Cove, believed to be on the site of a former Saxon settlement, can be traced back beyond Domesday Book of 1086. Then only a small hamlet in the Hundred of Crondall, it came under the tithing of Yateley for ecclesiastical purposes until St John's Church was built in 1844. However, its inclusion under the mantle of Farnborough does not deny its individual identity. Indeed, many inhabitants today vehemently defend their village status. There are many stories of the early rivalries between the two villages and local folklore would have it that passports were required to travel across their common boundaries! However, the fortunes of both Farnborough and Cove are inextricably intertwined so that photographic records of both places are to be found in this book.

The latter years of the 19th century saw a large number of private schools emerging in South Farnborough. Most of them had been converted from private houses and generally had extensive grounds for use as playing fields. The gravel terrain, with its top layer of sandy soil in that particular part of the town, provided good drainage which enabled sports to take place when school grounds in nearby towns were waterlogged. Perhaps that is why Farnborough schools excelled in county sporting events. Certainly sports and fitness were very high on the curriculum for pupils who were destined to go on to the top public schools in the country.

The dawn of the 20th century saw the final breakup of the manorial lands with the sale of the parkland surrounding the manor house. By that time, the occupant was no longer lord of the manor, that title having been sold off in the 1880s. Many new houses with large gardens were built in this prestigious part of the town known as Farnborough Park. Today, with ever increasing pressures on land availability, some of the larger gardens are being sold for building plots but the preservation of many beautiful old trees still reminds us of the glory of this former parkland.

In the south of the town, many of the earliest private residences have been demolished. Those that have survived generally have been converted into residential homes, have listed status or are in a Conservation area.

As the 20th century progressed, so did the development of the Balloon Factory which became the major employer in the town for the next fifty years. It took over a year to dismantle and remove the old balloon shed, gasometers and hydrogen generating plant from the Balloon Factory in Aldershot to their new home. This heavy transportation work was carried out with the aid of traction engines which, in the event, caused so much damage to the main road that the Army eventually received a hefty bill for repairs from the County Council. While rebuilding was in progress, a new airship shed was also erected.

Early experiments into military aeronautics were carried out for the War Office by the Royal Engineers, who had developed balloons for air observation. At the same time, Samuel Franklin Cody, an eccentric American showman, was experimenting with man-carrying kites and in 1906 he became Chief Instructor in 'Kiting' at the Balloon School. Cody wanted to add power to his kites but the War Office resisted as they felt the future lay only in airships. However, Cody continued to work on his flying machines until he achieved the first officially recorded powered flight, over Farnborough in 1908. Despite this achievement, the War Office ordered work on aeroplanes to stop because of the cost and the Factory continued to expand with airship construction. Nevertheless, progress in aeronautics could not be thwarted and in 1909 there was a reorganisation of the Factory to separate balloon construction from aircraft development. At that time 100 men and women were employed on the site.

From 1910 onwards experimentation in the air continued apace and all aspects of flying were tested. This research produced a wealth of scientific expertise in aeronautics which became world renowned. During the First World War, the workforce increased to around 5,000, bringing corresponding demands for accommodation. Many local houses were requisitioned and the Rafborough estate was built on the edge of the airfield. At the end of hostilities the workforce was dramatically reduced, causing economic hardship in the area. At the same time, following various name changes, the Factory became the Royal Aircraft Establishment.

Between the wars further research brought about the construction of wind tunnels and laboratories covering an increasing area of the common. Because of the important and secret nature of the work, the public was no longer allowed access. During the Second World War more than 6,000 people were employed there including many top scientists brought in from across the country. After the war half the workforce was again laid off but without the same economic implications as before because there was more employment to be found in other local businesses, many of which had developed through providing support services for the RAE. Nevertheless, housing was still proving to be a major problem and during the 1950s and 1960s vast areas on the northern edge of the town were developed to become the Fernhill and Hawley Estates.

This same period brought continued expansion at the RAE into world-leading supersonic research. Nevertheless, the increasing use of computer technology meant an eventual scaling down of manpower which then necessitated major rationalisation. Some of the experimental work was transferred from Farnborough and again a change of name coincided with a move to the western end of the airfield called Cody Park. The RAE became DERA and in 2003 was divided into the privatised QinetiQ, able to work in the commercial field, while the Defence Science and Technology Laboratory remained as part of the Ministry of Defence. This left a huge area of redundant buildings generally unsuitable for any alternative use. There was a great danger that our aeronautical heritage would disappear but fortunately, although much demolition has taken place, some of the most important buildings have been listed and retained. They are being incorporated into a new development on the site which, hopefully, will see the re-erection of an early airship shed as part of a wider scheme for commercial and community development with a hotel, shops and walkways. It is not reverting to common land but, after one hundred years, local people will again have access to part of an area once taken away from them. Much credit must go to the Farnborough Air Sciences Trust whose volunteers have worked tirelessly to ensure that not all of our aviation heritage has disappeared beneath the bulldozers.

Considering the importance of Farnborough's place in the story of aviation, it is sad that there are so few tangible monuments to the work of the early pioneers, many of whom lost their lives in the name of progress. Their work surely deserves greater recognition and it is hoped that the new heritage quarter will go some way to achieve this.

Alongside this redevelopment lies the airfield which was leased to TAG Aviation, who have heavily invested in a future dedicated to business flying. The facilities at this private airport have been upgraded to include a new control tower and servicing bays for aircraft. A whole new industry is emerging to cater for a world-class business airport serving the national and international private air traveller. An interesting bonus of this development is that once again the view across the airfield to the distant woodlands has been restored to what it was almost one hundred years ago.

The name of Farnborough is known throughout the world as the Home of the International Airshow. Staged in the town since the late 1940s, initially on an annual basis, it is now bi-annual and still draws enormous crowds to view its exhibits and flying displays. The show is staged over a number of days and brings a useful injection to the local economy, despite the gridlocked roads and additional noise generated by the flying. Even in a town that has lived under the flight path for so long there is still an air of excitement as the preparations for the show get under way and any patch of high ground in the vicinity still gets packed with eager spectators during the air display.

By the 1960s there was a decrease in military personnel and the shopping area of North Camp began to experience a gradual decline. Customers were also moving away from the High Street independent shops providing a personal service to the larger self service stores which could not be accommodated in the heavily built-up area of North Camp. A brand new shopping complex was built at Queensmead towards the northern end of town, which offered modern facilities where customers could shop beneath concrete canopies in a compact area. Considered to be the shopping centre of the future, it proved popular at first but rapid changes in shopping tastes quickly overtook it and customers began travelling further afield. The increased popularity of the motor car and the creation of out-of-town shopping malls has led to a re-think of the town's shopping requirements. Thus forty years on a regeneration scheme has been planned to create a more vibrant area where people can live, work and shop in accordance with modern ideas.

The building of the M3 motorway in the 1970s sealed Farnborough's position on the economic map. With good road and rail links, a history of technological expertise and a progressive building programme, Farnborough was an excellent place for aeronautical-related investment. Many financial and high-tech companies brought their headquarters to the town, providing good employment opportunities for the population.

The legacy of expertise in the aviation industry along with its strategic position within the transport network makes Farnborough an attractive location for continuing expansion. The town is currently undergoing great changes and the relentless march of progress threatens to bury our history beneath this increasing urbanisation. But all is not lost for ever.

The beginning of the 21st century has seen even more building and, with a finite amount of land in the town, it is inevitable that more demolition will take place. As memories fade and buildings disappear the photographic record becomes vital. I hope that the ensuing pages will bring back a wealth of memories for some, as well as providing future generations with an insight into their past. Each generation needs to have an understanding of the past in order that they may appreciate the present and be better able to safeguard the future.

One
North Farnborough

1 Farnborough Place, *c.*1950. This listed building, rebuilt in the late 1600s and now home to St Peter's Junior School, was owned by the lord of the manor until 1880, when the lordship was purchased by a local solicitor. Since that time the building has seen use as a private house, private school, nursing home, hotel and, immediately prior to its conversion into a junior school, it was owned by Power Jets Ltd who used it as an international jet turbine school. During the Farnborough Air Show, the staff took advantage of the superb view of the flying display which could be seen from the rooftop. It would appear that the rules for Health and Safety were not so stringent in those days as the spectators had to clamber up through a hatch in the roof.

2 The School was also home to the Consultancy Division of Power Jets (Research and Development) Ltd and in 1957 received a visit from Prince Philip. Mr T.G. Hicks, the Managing Director, is seen here presenting the Duke with a mounted turbine blade from the first Whittle jet engine. Mr J. Hodge, Chief Engineer, is on the extreme left and Mr C.E. Bell, the Patents Manager, is to the right of Mr Hicks.

3 This scene in the heart of the old village of Farnborough, now known as Farnborough Street, was photographed around one hundred years ago. The only difference today is that all the trees have gone and there is much more traffic. The Elm Tree on the far left was the centre of village life for many years and is recorded in the parish records in the mid-18th century. The farmhouse to the left, which used to be the old Street Farm, is now divided into four houses. Empress Cottages on the right were built in the late 19th century for people on the Farnborough Hill Estate.

4 Farnborough Hill Convent, 1954. The original house to the far right of the picture was erected by Thomas Longman, the publisher, in 1860 on the site of the earlier Windmill Hill. On his death it was purchased by the exiled Empress Eugénie of France, the widow of Napoleon III, who extended it by adding the cloisters with rooms above. The Empress died in 1920 and the Napoleon family eventually sold the house to Hillside Convent School. Subsequent additions enlarged the building with more classrooms and accommodation and, even at the time of writing, building work is under way on a new sports facility for the school.

This Certificate is presented by the Army Council, as a permanent record of their thanks, to be placed in the building which has been known and used as

The Empress Eugénie Hospital for British sick and wounded during the Great War, 1914-1919.

Winston S. Churchill

15th December, 1920.
The War Office,
London,

5 During the First World War, the Empress opened up part of Farnborough Hill as a hospital for wounded officers. Initially Lady Haig was the commandant but in 1915 Miss Isabel Vesey, daughter of General and Lady Vesey and a close friend of the Empress, took over until its closure in 1919. Today Vesey Close in Cove reminds us of the connection with the Empress. Dr Attenborough, who lived at The Ridges on the Farnborough Road, was Empress Eugénie's personal physician and he became the hospital surgeon.

6 The Empress died at the age of 94 on 11 July 1920 whilst on holiday in Spain. Her body was brought back by train to Farnborough Station to be buried in the crypt of St Michael's Abbey alongside her husband and her son. Her funeral was attended by King George V and Queen Mary as well as the royal heads of Spain and Portugal, together with high ranking representatives of other European countries.

7 The Empress had erected a small building (just visible on the left of plate 4) where some of the imperial treasures were kept. These included the State Carriage, shown here, and the Prince Imperial's uniform, medals and sword.

8 Highgate Lane in the 1930s. This lane was originally called Heath Gate Lane when it connected the old village to the heathland beyond the Farnborough Road. These houses were built by local builder Mr W. J. Rumble. This is on the corner of the western end of Chingford Avenue and was where the late Empress had crossed to gain access to Church Path (bottom right out of view) on her regular walks to St Michael's Abbey. The only basic differences in the scene today are modern lamp posts and numerous television aerials.

9 St Michael's Abbey in the 1920s. Situated on a hill immediately across the railway from Farnborough Hill, it was erected by the Empress Eugénie as a resting place for her late husband, the Emperor Napoleon III and her son, the Prince Imperial. The railway runs through a deep cutting beyond and in the distance can be seen the driveway winding up to Farnborough Hill. The late Empress used to walk down through the grounds, crossing the railway footbridge on Church Path, and in through a private gateway which led her directly to the mausoleum.

10 The Clockhouse, probably the most famous landmark in Farnborough, was erected in 1895 by Henry Dever, the Chairman of the Council. When this photograph was taken in 1905 it was a private house surrounded by trees, on the junction of Victoria Road and Hillfield Road, where they join the Farnborough Road. Since those days the building has undergone little visible change except that the cupola was lowered in the 1950s because the columns were rotten. It became an estate agent's on the ground floor in the 1930s with the upstairs being used as a tea room. It still is an estate agent's today but the tea room has gone and the tranquillity of the surroundings has given way to the bustle of the busiest roundabout in town. With the disappearance of the fields behind, Hillfield Road has become Clockhouse Road.

11 The *Chudleigh Hotel*, seen here in 1971, was built as a private house on Victoria Road, near the Clockhouse. It was used as an unofficial outpost of the RAE, nicknamed The Chudleigh Mess, during the First World War. It had been requisitioned by the Government and made available to F.M. Green, the engineer in charge of designs at the RAE. He arranged for the house to be furnished sufficiently to accommodate eight or nine of the up-and-coming scientific graduates brought in to work at the RAE. The 'Mess' was an important bolt-hole away from the stresses of working on the pressing problems in aeronautics in the First World War. F.M. Green in an article written in 1958 recalled that, of those who were involved, three became peers of the realm, five became knights, three won Nobel Prizes and many became professors or Fellows of the Royal Society. After the war, it became the home of General Ravenhill and in recent times was demolished and replaced by a residential development named Chudleigh Court. There is still a vestige of the old property left in some stone steps which give pedestrian access from Victoria Road.

12 Barnaboys in Church Avenue was built in 1909 by the Hobbs family. Lt Col P.J.B. Hobbs, later to become Major General Hobbs, was posted to Aldershot in 1901 when he became Chief Instructor at the Army Service Corps School of Instruction. He purchased a large plot of land in Farnborough Park and had this house erected by a Farnham builder, in 1906. In this photograph the beautifully laid out croquet lawn gives a glimpse of those far off days of the early 20th century when house parties were an important part of the social scene. Gen. Hobbs had served with Earl Haig in the First World War and the visitor's book from the house shows that after the Earl's death his son, the new Earl, continued to visit. Another frequent visitor was General Hobbs' only son, Carleton P. Hobbs, the famous radio actor from the golden years of radio, who was born in Farnborough in 1898. A very popular actor, his most famous role was as Sherlock Holmes in a production for BBC's Children's Hour, which he went on to play in the adult version for over 17 years. Like many of the very large houses, it is impractical for a family home today, and has been divided into several separate residences, and part of the large garden has been built upon.

13 When the Empress Eugénie died in 1920, the Farnborough Hill Estate was left to her nephew, Prince Victor Napoleon and his wife Princess Clementine. When Princess Clementine died in 1926, Farnborough Hill itself was purchased by the nuns for the use of Hillside Convent, but the balance of the land on the west of Farnborough Road was sold for redevelopment as the Empress Estate. All the roads in this residential area have names which are connected to the Empress. This house in Empress Avenue was built by Wm Fleetwood of Canterbury Road in the early 1930s. Some slight changes have taken place since then but it is still easily recognisable. The painters in the white overalls are Mr Fred Roberts on the left and his son, Harry, on the right.

14 After the Second World War there was a big demand for new houses but materials were in short supply and licences to build were limited. Nevertheless, because of its unique situation in having a large number of former RAE workers laid off after the war, the Council was allowed to build more than the normal allotted number. Large tracts of land to the north east of the town were earmarked for Council Housing and many new homes were erected by Wimpey on the Hawley and Fox Lane Estates in the 1950s. On a cold wet day in 1953, members of the Council were photographed inspecting one of the first of those houses. Left to right are: Mrs Andrewartha, W. Needham, W. Woolger, ?, W. Hitchcock, ?, W. Perry, ?, ?, Mrs Mosses, I. Jenkins, Mrs White, J. White, ?, ?, ?.

15 Queensmead, early 1960s. This state-of-the-art new concept in shopping was opened in the late 1950s when the shopping facilities in the southern part of the town began to go into decline. This was partly due to the reduction in the military population but was also influenced by a change in people's shopping habits. The shoppers wanted self-service stores and the ability to keep dry. In those days one could drive through the shopping centre, park outside the shops and keep dry under the concrete canopies.

16 By 1977, when this photograph was taken, Queensmead had been pedestrianised and enlarged by the addition of the adjoining Kingsmead to the east. At the time of writing whole tracts of Queensmead have been boarded up awaiting redevelopment and it is hard to imagine that this landscaped and well illuminated area could once have looked so inviting. It is hoped that the plans for the regeneration of that area will soon be implemented.

Two

South Farnborough

17 Knellwood Residential Home, 1961. This lovely Victorian house was built by William Knell, an early land developer, who purchased large tracts of land sold off by the lord of the manor in the 1860s. In its former days this was a private residence where garden parties were often held in the beautiful grounds. For some years it saw service as a hotel until it was turned into a residential home in 1947 to become the town's war memorial for those who had fallen in the Second World War. The house today has been greatly extended and the chimneys have gone, but it still retains the grandeur of former times and provides a tranquil setting for those who reside there.

18 The Farnborough & Cove War Memorial Cottage Hospital in Albert Road was opened in 1921 by Earl Haig, as a memorial to the men of Farnborough and Cove who fell in the First World War. It had 12 beds and a private ward. In 1933, the North Farnborough Nursing Home, housed in Farnborough Place, closed, necessitating more bed space in the cottage hospital and a new wing was built accommodating an operating theatre and X-ray room. It was opened by Countess Haig on 7 July 1934.

Farnborough Hospital Week

May 6th to May 12th 1945

FARNBOROUGH AND COVE
WAR MEMORIAL
COTTAGE HOSPITAL.

4th June, 1945.

DEAR SIR OR MADAM,

The response given by the people of FARNBOROUGH to the HOSPITAL WEEK has exceeded the highest expectations.

Although no target figure was named it is very pleasing indeed to record that a sum of over £2,000, clear of expenses, has been added to the Hospital Funds.

The combined efforts of our townsfolk have brought about the magnificent result, in which I feel is embodied many expressions of gratitude and joy at the cessation of the EUROPEAN WAR, which happened to take place during the week.

It would be impossible to write and thank everyone who helped with gifts, money and work, but everyone can be assured that everything they did is highly valued and demonstrates how much our Hospital and Maternity Unit are dear to the hearts of us all.

This sum of money will help the Committee to embark upon some of the extensions which are contemplated.

Yours sincerely,

W. H. BARNES,
Chairman of Committee.

19 During the Second World War, the hospital set aside a number of beds for air-raid casualties. In the event, there was little enemy action locally so the beds were not fully utilised but the hospital received a small income from the Ministry in compensation for loss of revenue. Nevertheless, as the hospital was funded entirely by voluntary support, the running costs were an ever-present problem. The League of Friends worked very hard and many fund-raising activities were held, including a dance at the Town Hall and annual street collections. In 1945 there was a bumper street collection which coincided with the cessation of the war.

20 In the 1950s a pageant at the Town Hall depicted 'Nursing through the Ages' and Sister Lowrey is seen here outside the hospital dressed as Nurse Edith Cavell.

21 Matron Lowrey and the Chairman of the Management Committee cutting the first turf when building work commenced on the extension for the new out-patients and casualty department in 1962. This brought forth an anonymous ditty:

> Here is the sod that Matron did dig,
> eight inches square that's not very big!
> This poor little worm nearly met his fate
> and became a victim of the Welfare State.

The hospital became redundant when Frimley Park Hospital opened in the early 1970s. The old hospital is now a short-stay facility and day-care centre under the name of Devereux House.

22 The Maternity Unit at Farley House used to hold annual baby parties for the families and here in the mid-1950s Matron N. Ralph on the right is seen with Lady Haining, and Mr Collier who is holding a microphone in one hand and a bouncing baby in the other. Sister Lowrey and Sister Arch are on the left.

23 Arnold House No 2, 1912. These three large houses in Southampton Street were known as Gosfield, Mayhill and Shalmsford. They were on the opposite side of the road to Arnold House which itself sits on the apex of Farnborough Road and Southampton Street. Lying directly across the road from the airfield, Arnold House once housed a school and then, during the early days of the 20th century, many of the early test pilots lived there. Gosfield was used as an unofficial Mess run by F. M. Green and Edward Busk and was given the name Arnold House No 2. Shalmsford was the original house and surgery for Dr Hunter Dunn, who subsequently moved to his more famous house in Reading Road which featured in John Betjeman's poem 'The Subaltern's Love Song'.

24 The Warren, Southampton Street when it was put up for sale in 1930, having previously been in the tenancy of a major in the army. This double-fronted house with the spherical ornamentation on the eaves is typical of the speculative building which took place in this part of South Farnborough in the late 19th century. The demolition of the house in the late 1980s, along with its neighbour to the left, caused a great uproar among local people as there was a fear that re-development would alter the character of the road. The whole area was then designated a Conservation area and the developer had to rebuild the houses in exactly the same style to be in keeping with the Victorian street scene.

25 All the roads in this part of the town are wide and tree-lined, based on a design by an architect named Currie who helped to set out the road system of South Farnborough in the 1860s. This scene in Netley Street, which adjoins Southampton Street, is little changed today, save that the trees are much more mature and there are roundabouts at each junction.

26 Stirling Villa was one of three pairs of large three-storey semi-detached houses built on Alexandra Road in the mid-1860s by Mr Chatfield, another early land developer. Two of the houses have recently been refurbished and are now divided into apartments.

27 St Mark's Church was built on the junction of Reading and Alexandra Roads in 1881. This photograph taken in 1905 commemorates their Rose Bazaar, a successful fund-raising event held in the Town Hall opposite, when roses were the dominant theme.

28 St Mark's, in its position near the airfield, took on the role as the place of worship for the Royal Flying Corps and its successor, the Royal Air Force. After the First World War, the Lady Chapel was dedicated to the airmen who had given their lives for their country. The chapel walls are lined with oak panels and plaques bearing the names of all the servicemen who are commemorated. Outside, a war memorial and seats were erected on the corner, as seen here in 1922. These were subsequently removed in the 1960s across the road to church land on the corner of Alexandra and Guildford Roads when a roundabout was built at this six-way junction.

29 This view of Alexandra Road, taken in 1950, on a lovely sunny afternoon, shows the Post Office which was opened in the late 1930s. The pine trees and the bus shelter beneath them were soon to disappear to make way for the municipal gardens in front of the Town Hall.

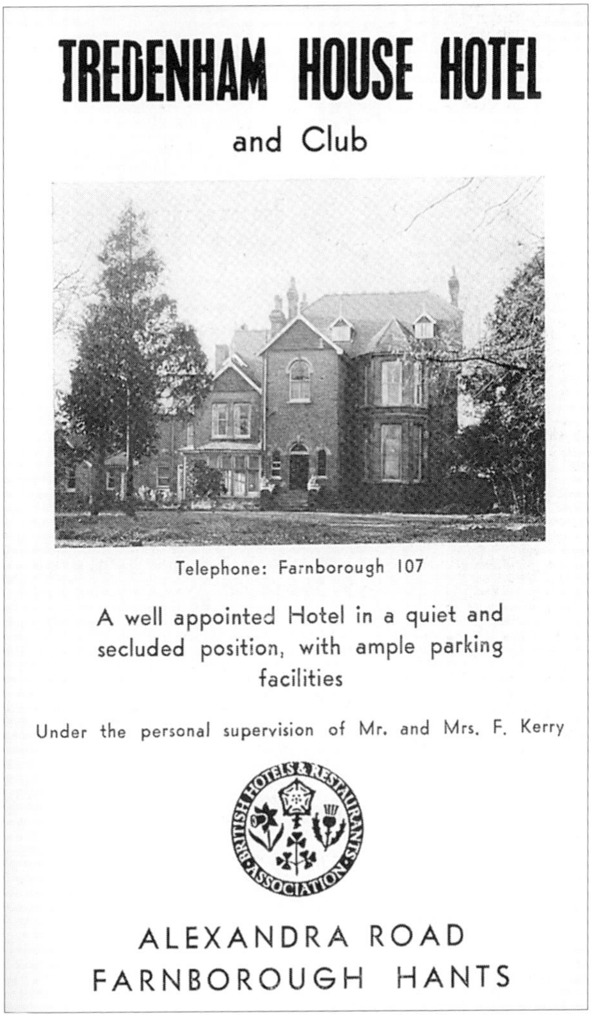

30 Many large houses became too expensive to run as private homes and were put to other uses. Tredenham House, between Alexandra Road and Winchester Street, was built by Colonel Carlyon in the late 19th century. It was used as a school in the 1930s and this advert from 1961 shows a popular hotel and club used by many of the local organisations as their meeting place. When it was demolished it was replaced by a development of town houses called Tredenham Close. The original lodge to the house still exists on Alexandra Road and is home to a Chinese restaurant.

31 The original fire station in Farnborough was a shed in Camp Road in the late 19th century. Early in the 20th century it moved to new premises at the rear of Farnborough Town Hall. By 1960 it had moved again to this building in Reading Road, where the photograph was taken in 1970. Today the fire station is a modern building on Lynchford Road opposite the end of Osborne Road.

32 Farnborough Fire Brigade, 1960. Left to right: back row—A. Dawes, R. Dudman, R. Williams, R. Wilkinson, M. Poulter, D. DeVigne; middle row—G. Adams, P. Reynolds, T. Francis, D. Dawes, G. Dunne; front row—F. Dunn, G. Smith, F. Cook, R. S. Barnes, A. Dewhurst, W. Bowen.

Three
North Camp

33 Lynchford Road, on an unusually quiet day in 1915 for this very busy road bordering the military North Camp. John Drew the stationers in the forefront is displaying numerous fancy goods including toys, books, postcards and a child's kite very similar to the ones which Samuel Cody had been using for experimental flying only a few years earlier. The shop on the left is Litchfields the chemist and on the right is Dormer the draper, next to Darracotts the baker, who also served lunches and teas. All along the road there were many teashops frequented by the large number of military families in the vicinity.

34 Brother Ernest Litchfield, of Farnborough and North Camp Masonic Lodge No 2203, here shown in 1898 in his regalia as Past Provincial Assistant Grand Director of Ceremonies. He was manager of a chemist's shop on the corner of Church Path and Lynchford Road in 1891 and took over the ownership a few years later. It is still a chemists and, although it has been modernised, some of the original shop fittings have been retained to give us a nostalgic glimpse of the past.

35 Thomas White & Co., *c.*1910. On the corner of Camp and Lynchford Roads, this was a very popular department store until it closed in the 1950s. It was originally built as a wooden structure in the 1860s, rebuilt in 1897 and, having suffered fire damage over the years, was totally rebuilt again in the late 20th century to give us the austere building we have today. In its heyday it employed a large number of staff, and people still talk fondly about a style of shopping which has long since disappeared.

36 The Avenue Electric Theatre was opened in Camp Road in December 1911. Cinemas were in their infancy but the proprietors, The Associated Electric Theatres Ltd, based in London's Charing Cross Road, felt that there was great potential with the military presence in North Camp. As a picture playhouse, it staged dramatic plays as well as the latest films in its very luxurious surroundings where tickets ranged from one shilling for a reservation in the circle to 3d and 6d for the stalls. In the photograph, the manager, Mr C. Cook, is to the left of the camera. The Theatre closed in the 1930s but was reopened as a cinema for the Canadian servicemen who were stationed locally during the Second World War. It became Woolworths in the 1950s but eventually became derelict and the site has now been redeveloped.

37 This shop in Somerset Road, opposite the St John Ambulance Hall, was owned by Mrs Harriet Knight when this photograph was taken in *c.*1930. In days gone by there were many small shops in residential streets which just served the people in the immediate vicinity. The shop was often a converted front room with living accommodation behind and upstairs. Many of the items displayed are very familiar today, such as Rowntree's Cocoa, Lux, Brooke Bond Tea, Oxo and Bisto. The shop survived into the 1980s but has now been re-converted into a house.

38 Mr A. Hewett originally had a butcher's shop in Queen's Road and in 1915 he moved to these premises in Lynchford Road, near the *North Camp Hotel*. By 1934, when this photograph was taken, he employed a number of butchers including Mr Harry Worgan, second from the left, who was also a slaughterman at Mr Hewett's slaughterhouse in Peabody Road. Mr Hewett is fourth from the right with Mr Lou Hankins next right.

39 This prize animal was purchased at Guildford Market by Mr Hewett, bowler-hatted on the right, and donated for the ox roast held in the town in 1937 to celebrate the coronation of King George VI. The photograph is taken just inside the entrance to the slaughterhouse in Peabody Road. The man in overalls is Mr Harry Worgan.

40 Goble Stores was in Peabody Road, opposite the slaughterhouse. In the early years of the 20th century it was owned by Mrs Chitty and then taken over by the Goble family. Mr Goble, whose name is on the gate, also ran his building company from the premises. The gentleman in the photograph, taken in 1964, is Mr Joe Oliver, a council employee who is proudly showing off the new Council gully emptier that he drove. The attachment on the front below the radiator grille is a fixing for a snowplough.

41 The International Stores in Lynchford Road, *c.*1953. Many of the nationally known shops opened branches locally which indicates what a thriving shopping area it once was. The store subsequently moved into Camp Road to become one of the first self-service grocers in the area and eventually transferred to Queensmead. The staff lined up behind the counter are, left to right: Joan Croft, Daphne Barham, Manager Mr Oliver, Assistant Manager Peter Nash, William Crew, Gladys Williams, Joyce Bailey, Eileen McGrath and Barbara Frost.

42 This view of Lynchford Road photographed in 1915 is looking westwards. On the right is the International Tea Company, later to become International Stores. The three-storey building in the centre is Turners, on the corner of Peabody Road, with The Corn Stores on the opposite corner. The Corn Stores was owned by Mr Clement Yates, whose father, Reuben Yates, opened the first shop in Lynchford Road.

43 Mr Clement Yates as Chairman of the Farnborough Urban District Council in 1908-9. He was born in the house his father built next door to the *Blacksmiths Arms*, which is now the *Elephant and Castle*. He took over the family forage and corn merchant business when his father died in 1886. All the adjacent buildings on that corner were once owned by the Yates family, giving the name of Yates Yard to a little group of cottages at the rear in what is now Peabody Road Car Park.

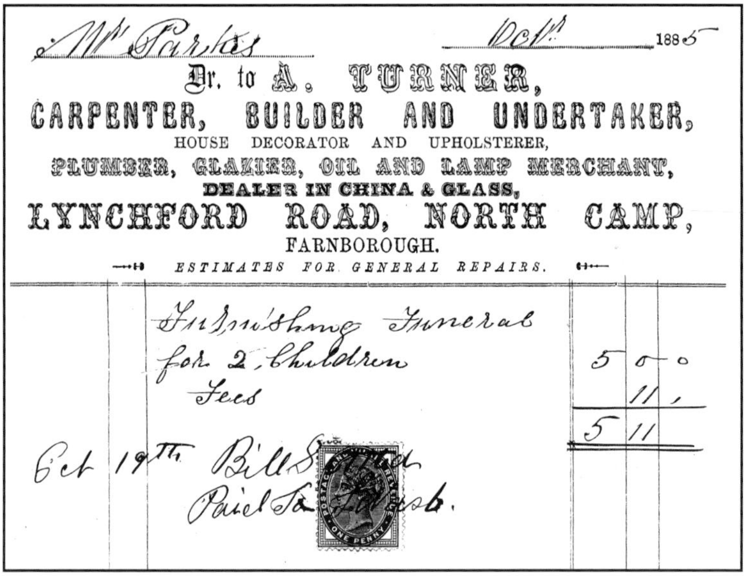

Mr Parkes Octr 1885

Dr. to A. TURNER,

CARPENTER, BUILDER AND UNDERTAKER,

HOUSE DECORATOR AND UPHOLSTERER,

PLUMBER, GLAZIER, OIL AND LAMP MERCHANT,

DEALER IN CHINA & GLASS,

LYNCHFORD ROAD, NORTH CAMP,

FARNBOROUGH.

ESTIMATES FOR GENERAL REPAIRS.

Furnishing Funeral for 2 Children	5	0	0
Fees		11	
	5	11	

Oct 19th Bill Settled
Paid

44 Mr A. Turner set up his business in 1872 and for many years was the Garrison Undertaker as well as a carpenter, builder, house decorator and general merchants. This bill for the funeral of two children of the Parkes family illustrates the diversity of his business.

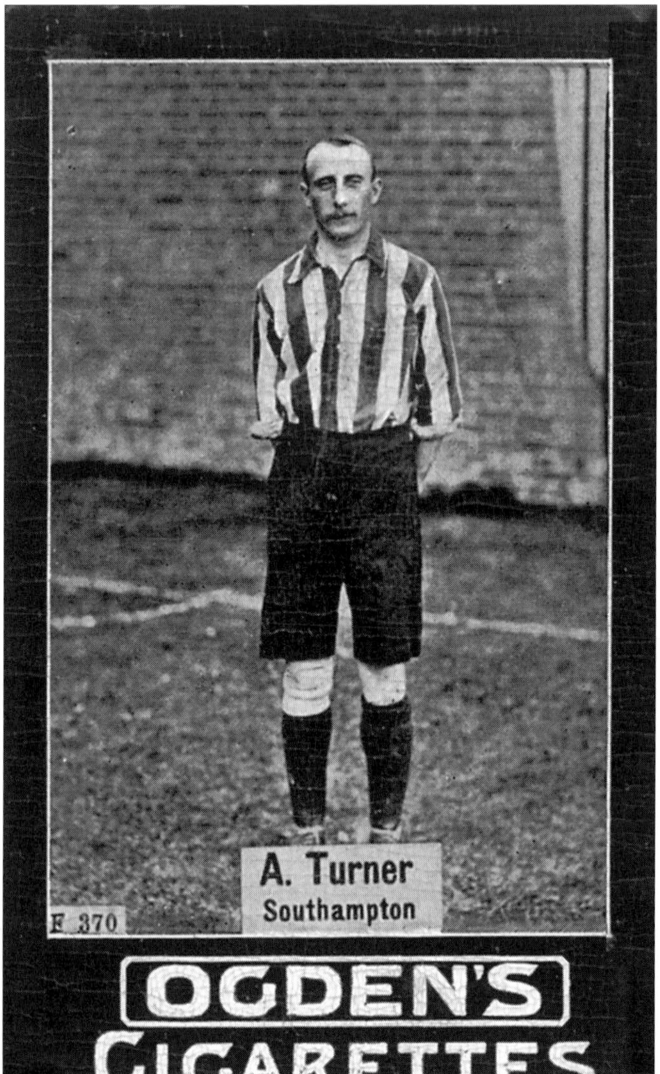

45 Mr Turner's son, Arthur, known as Archie, achieved fame on a cigarette card with his prowess as a footballer. Born in Farnborough, he played for Aldershot and then South Farnborough before joining Southampton as an outside right. He was 23 when he won his two caps and went on to Derby County where he had 21 Football League appearances. Then followed spells at Newcastle United and Tottenham Hotspur before he returned to Southampton in 1904. His career took him to 78 Southern League matches and 20 FA Cup appearances. He retired from full-time football in 1905 and returned to his father's business. He continued to play football and cricket locally until he died in 1925.

46 There was plenty of business for photographers in the early days of the 20th century. Mr J. Thomson had a large shop and studio at No 2 The Pavement, Lynchford Road, photographed here in 1909. The backs of his photographs indicate royal patronage including The Dukes of York, Connaught and Cambridge, who were all, at one time, serving locally in the army. The shops on The Pavement were built on the edge of a gravel pit and in the early days so much gravel had been dug out for the nearby roads that these buildings had to be built with basements. The old gravel pit accounts for the steep slope into the adjacent Morris Road and the naming of Gravel Road nearby to the east.

47 Southern Lynchford Road, 1920s. The houses in this section of Lynchford Road, which leads down to North Camp Station, have hardly changed at all with Lynchford Terrace on the left, and St James' Villas on the right just before Park Road. This stretch of road is now a cul-de-sac, with a new road immediately to the south which connects with the roundabout leading to the Blackwater Valley Relief Road.

48 The *Fir Tree Inn*, seen here in 1998 not long after the last pint had been drawn, was built in 1862 and became a very popular beerhouse with the soldiers in North Camp. Very near to North Camp station, it was reputed to have been a ticket office for the old horse-drawn trams which linked North Camp station with the main-line station at the other end of town. Falling business led to its demise, not helped by the construction of the Blackwater Valley Relief Road between it and the rest of the town.

Chapter Four
Cove

49 In the early 1840s, the people of Cove decided they would like their own church in the village rather than have to travel to Yateley or Farnborough to worship. Built in what was then the centre of a small agricultural village, the church of St John the Baptist was consecrated in 1844. This postcard dated 1934 carries a message from the sender who had just arrived in the village. He comments on the fact that there are very few cars to be seen, the roads are quite rough and everyone seems to travel by bicycle.

50 This house, originally called Cove Court, was erected in Minley Road near St John's Church on the site of the former Fuller's Farm. It was built as the vicarage about the same time as the church and had extensive gardens, as can be seen in this photograph of 1914. Inside the house was some beautiful black oak panelling, thought to have come from Winchester Cathedral, and some large chalk fireplaces. The steps to the cellar were believed to be those in the original farmhouse. Today, the house has long since gone and the grounds have been developed into Shakespeare Gardens.

51 Just round the corner from the church is the *Plough & Horses* on the corner of Fleet Road and St John's Road as it was in the 1930s. Built in the late 1800s, it was originally called *The Plough*. The oak tree on the right has grown considerably and there is still a pillar box in the same position today.

52 The Ball family outside their house by West Heath railway bridge, *c.*1910. The house, which used to be known as Wright's, is one of a pair on the northern side of the bridge. The railway embankment beside a smaller bridge than today can be seen in the background on the left.

53 *The Anchor Inn*, 1930s. This view, taken when it was leased by Simonds Brewery, shows the old company sign of the hop leaf on the left. It is recorded that there was a building in Cove in the 1600s called the Anchor but the present building, now renamed The Old Courthouse, dates from the early 1800s. In earlier days it was used both for vestry meetings and as a local courthouse. Much of the surrounding meadow land once belonged to the Anchor and many local fairs and horticultural shows were held in what was known as Anchor or Gosden's Meadow, after a former owner.

54 This very early photograph of a cab with the buggy seat at the rear was taken outside the *Anchor* at the end of the 19th century. Many inns used to operate what we would today call a taxi service and this cab is being driven by Mr William Grenham who owned the *Alma* next door.

55 In the 1891 census Mr Grenham is listed as a filly proprietor and his business was thriving when this photograph was taken *c.*1900. He was a favourite coachman of the Empress Eugénie and he used to take his cab to meet passengers from Farnborough railway station. He is seen here driving one of his carriages, with another much larger one in the adjacent stable yard.

56 William Grenham's son, Frank, also worked in the business and, as a child, he used to take people to North Camp in his pony and trap. By the early 1920s the horse and carriage had given way to a smart new motor taxi seen here with Frank at the wheel. Frank was well known in the licensed trade and eventually moved on, first to the *Imperial Arms* in Farnborough Street, and then to the *Alexandra* in Victoria Road, Farnborough, leaving his father to carry on at the *Alma*. Comparison with photograph 71 shows that the stables has now lost its original thatched roof.

57 This Cove street scene, taken in 1931, is in what had then become the commercial heart of the village and shows the *Alma* and the *Anchor* on the right, with the *Tradesmen's Arms* on the left and the then recently built Methodist church centre left. The new, more formal Simonds signs have now appeared on the *Alma*. Sadly, the *Alma* has since disappeared to become the car park to The Old Courthouse.

58 The foundation stone of the new Methodist church shown in the previous photograph was laid on August bank holiday in 1924. The architect was Mr A. H. Dungay of Farnborough and the building was completed the following year. The old church had been built in 1888, but it is believed there was an even earlier chapel on the site dating from around 1800. This photograph, taken before the foundation stone was laid in 1924, shows the house next door, which had to be demolished to make way for the new church. The 1924 church has in turn been replaced by a more modern church, opened in 1984.

59 One of the pub games that seems to have died out is Shoveha'penny where an old-style half-penny was 'shoved' along a flat board by a smart slap with the palm of the hand. The *Alma* Darts and Shoveha'penny team have obviously been successful some time around 1930 when they posed for this photograph. From left to right, back row: ? Roberts, Harry Sylvester, Arthur Budd, ?, Jack Kite, ?, Ollie Girling, ?; seated: Algie Harvey, Starry May, Dick Coles (bowler hat), Henry Chard, William Grenham (centre), Reg Williams, ? Wise, Dick Dastable, Dick Lee.

60 In 1964, the *Alma* closed down and the licence was transferred to a new public house in Prospect Road called *The Thatched Cottage*. Originally a two-room, 18th-century, timber-framed cottage, it was extended to double its size in the 1930s by Cmdr J.N. Sparks, a prominent Farnborough councillor. This photograph was taken in 1960. Eventually it was purchased by Courage's Brewery, the successors to Simonds, and turned into what is now an established pub on the edge of the West Heath Estate.

61 School Treat, 1914. The annual school treat was a very popular day out for the children in the Cove schools. This postcard shows upward of 500 children marching past Mr T. Moore's grocery shop in Cove Street to take part in the games on Cove Green. The children had started off from Mr Gosden's meadow behind the *Anchor* and, after their activities on the Green, they all ended up in Mr Yeoman's meadow for tea.

62 Cove Green 1914. There are a few umbrellas visible but obviously the weather was not bad enough to deter the enjoyment of the youngsters taking part in the races. The Green also provided a popular venue for Billy Matthews' fairground rides from North Camp.

63 Mr James Cook's grocery store in Tower Hill in the 1930s. To judge by the signs, he sold at least four different brands of tea at around 6d. or 7d. a quarter-pound packet. On the side of the building is an advert for the newly opened Scala Cinema in North Camp. Mr A. Cook took over the business until it was sold to become a wool and fancy goods shop, later demolished to enlarge the Tower Hill Garage site.

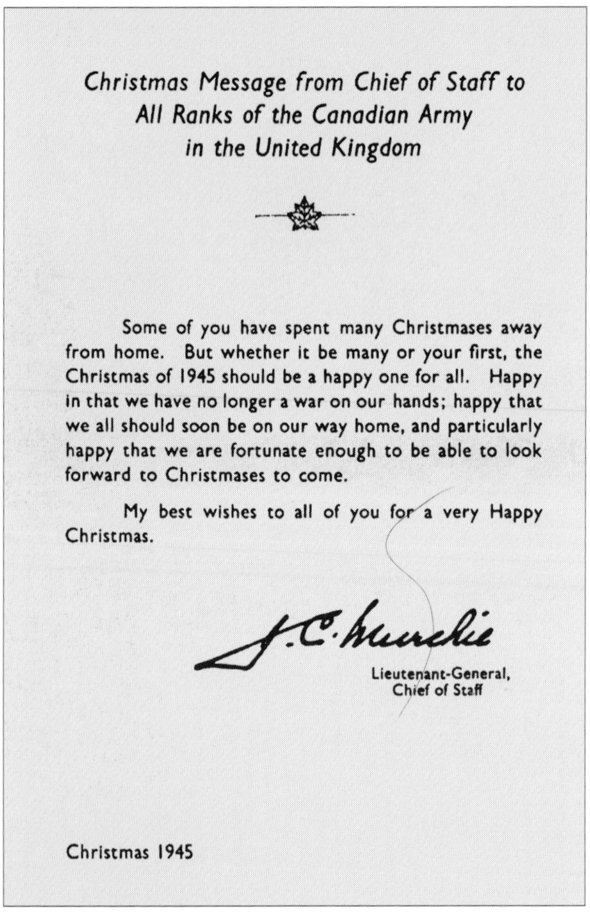

Christmas Message from Chief of Staff to All Ranks of the Canadian Army in the United Kingdom

Some of you have spent many Christmases away from home. But whether it be many or your first, the Christmas of 1945 should be a happy one for all. Happy in that we have no longer a war on our hands; happy that we all should soon be on our way home, and particularly happy that we are fortunate enough to be able to look forward to Christmases to come.

My best wishes to all of you for a very Happy Christmas.

J. C. Murchie

Lieutenant-General,
Chief of Staff

Christmas 1945

64 During the Second World War everyone was encouraged to recycle materials for use in the war effort. The schools of Cove and Farnborough took part in a competition to see which school could collect the most scrap iron and in 1943 the winner was Cove Senior School. So enthusiastic were the children in their collecting that, on more than one occasion, perfectly good items mysteriously disappeared from their homes and ended up on this heap.

65 During both world wars, thousands of Canadians served alongside British forces and many were stationed locally. Their presence made quite a difference to the lives of the local youngsters; they brought with them a plentiful supply of chocolate and sweets, which were on ration here, and they monopolised the girls at the regular village dances. In 1945, when peace was declared in Europe, arrangements were made for the Canadians to be repatriated to their own country. As a farewell gesture of gratitude for the hospitality given by the local people, lavish Christmas parties were held for all the local children. At one party in Cove over 1,000 children attended. The Canadians themselves were also treated to a celebration Christmas Dinner when this message of thanks for their contribution to the war effort was given by the Chief of Staff. (See the inside back cover for the signed menu.)

SALVAGE
YOU MAY WIN THE LEAGUE BUT WHAT ABOUT
KICKED OFF 1ST MARCH
THE NATIONAL WASTE PAPER CONTEST?
FULL TIME 31ST MAY
GET WEAVING COVE!
PUT
OUT
THAT
WASTE
PAPER

66 Rivalry between Cove and Farnborough has been going on for generations, and here in 1948 the traders of Cove are encouraging the village to beat Farnborough in their efforts at collecting salvage for recycling. The national recovery from the war was being severely held back because of the shortage of paper, so this contest offered prizes to the towns and villages with the best results. Farnborough was obviously doing well in the football league but whether Cove won this local spat is not recorded. Nevertheless, the aggregate of the two towns topped the previous year by eight tons.

67 The women's Bright Hour group met regularly at the Methodist church and here is the 1957 group in front of the old 1924 building. When the new church was opened in 1984, the old buildings were retained for community use, but have since been demolished. Among the ladies present are: Mesdames F. Yeomans, Annie Cleeves, Thompson, Hall, Lea, Willis, Morgan, Spreadborough, Edwards and Bell; the Misses Street, New and Waters, together with the Rev. Charles Deakin, Rev. Bernard Palmer and Rev. W.R. Kent.

Five

Railway Lines

68 Farnborough railway station, 1840. This lithograph shows the view from the western side looking towards the Farnborough road. The cutting through the hill beyond gives an indication of the scale of digging out that was required to bring the railway through from Woking. The line to Gosport was completed that same year and by 1844 the railway buildings at Farnborough had more than doubled.

69 This lithograph of 1844 shows Queen Victoria arriving to greet King Louis Philippe of Spain who had come to visit her at Windsor. Because there was no railway station at Windsor, the Queen used Farnborough when travelling to London or to her home on the Isle of Wight. The facilities at the station were far in excess of those normally provided for a small village station, but they were specifically designed for the use of royal visitors.

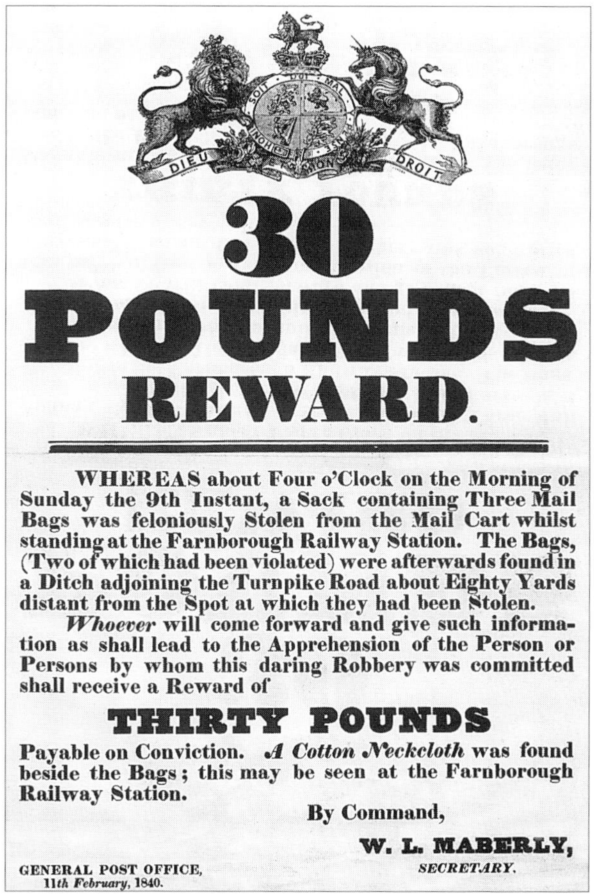

30 POUNDS REWARD.

WHEREAS about Four o'Clock on the Morning of Sunday the 9th Instant, a Sack containing Three Mail Bags was feloniously Stolen from the Mail Cart whilst standing at the Farnborough Railway Station. The Bags, (Two of which had been violated) were afterwards found in a Ditch adjoining the Turnpike Road about Eighty Yards distant from the Spot at which they had been Stolen.

Whoever **will come forward and give such information as shall lead to the Apprehension of the Person or Persons by whom this daring Robbery was committed shall receive a Reward of**

THIRTY POUNDS

Payable on Conviction. ***A Cotton Neckcloth*** **was found beside the Bags; this may be seen at the Farnborough Railway Station.**

By Command,

W. L. MABERLY,
SECRETARY.

GENERAL POST OFFICE,
***11th February*, 1840.**

70 The Post Office quickly took advantage of this speedier form of transport and began despatching letters by train. The highway robbers of the day were also quick to turn their attentions from stagecoach to mail cart.

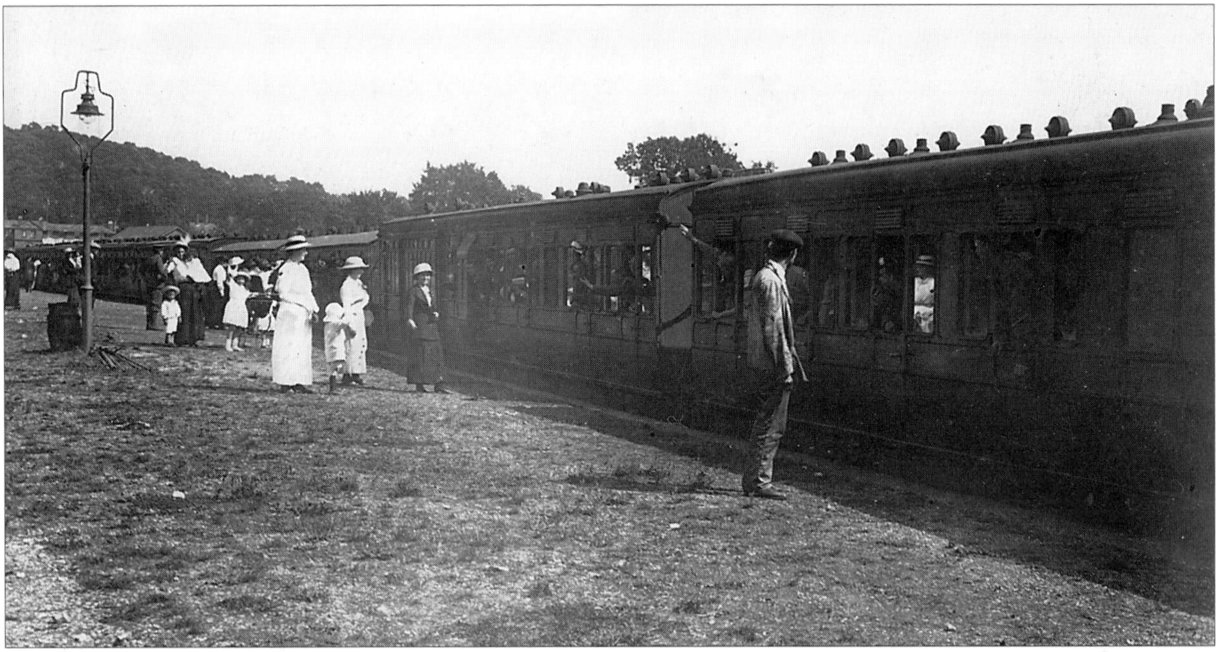

71 From the time the army arrived to build their camp in Aldershot in 1853 until well into the 20th century, Farnborough saw a vast amount of troops passing through the station. During the Crimean War thousands of wounded men returned from the front to make their way to North Camp. Even when Aldershot opened a station in 1870, Farnborough was used in preference because it had direct access to the coast. Here in 1914, this train standing at the military platform is full to capacity with soldiers off to war.

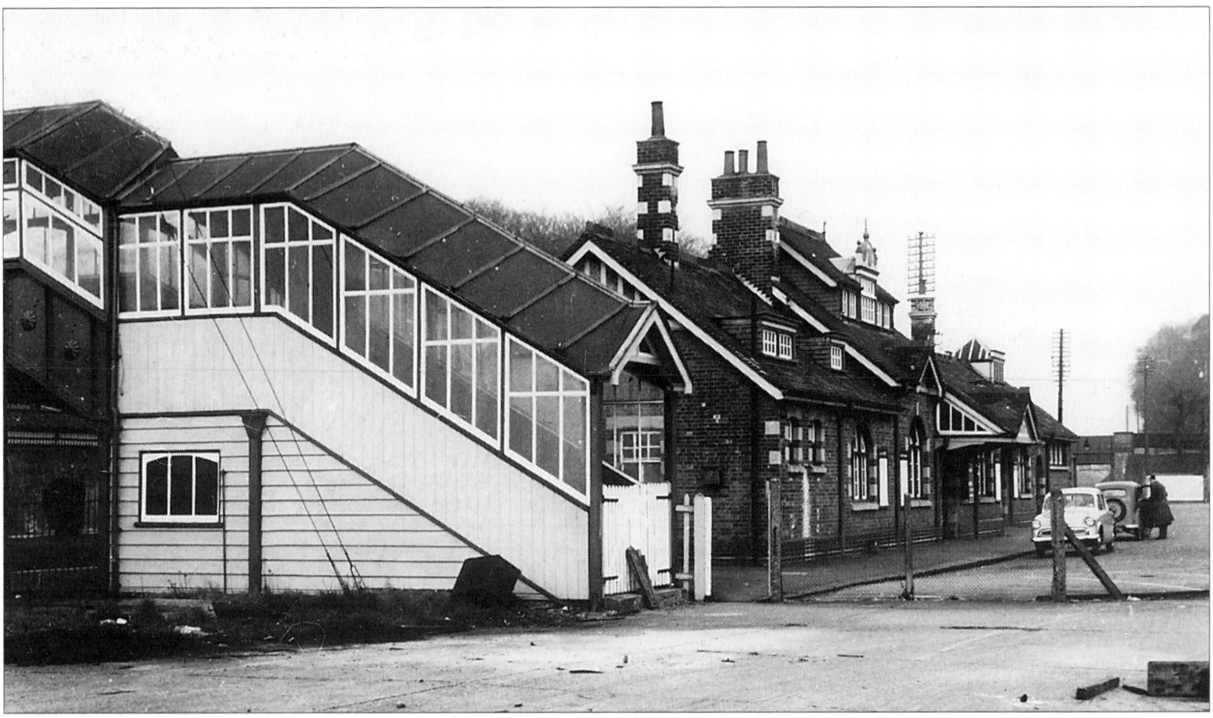

72 Farnborough station, 1960. Those were the days when passengers could still cross the railway lines via a covered bridge. Nowadays there is no roof on the bridge and it can only be accessed from inside the station. The very grand station of the 19th century gave way to this smaller version when the lines were increased from two to four at the beginning of the 20th century. This extremely busy station is now dwarfed by surrounding office blocks, but its general appearance remains much the same.

73 Train crash, 1947. One man was killed and five seriously injured when two trains collided on the straight stretch of line approaching West Heath Bridge from Fleet. An express train was waiting at signals when another express crashed into the back of it. The accident was partly due to a power failure causing loss of communication with the signal boxes.

74 The engine of the second train was derailed and the wreckage was strewn over all four of the tracks. After working all through the night, workmen cleared two of the lines by next morning and normal service was resumed within two days.

75 Farnborough's second railway station is now called Farnborough North and is on the Reading to Guildford line which was opened in 1849. Originally a small wooden hut served as the station premises. Today all these buildings, including the signal box, have disappeared to be replaced by modern shelters. The crossing gates still take pedestrians through to nearby Frimley Green across the Blackwater River, although it is no longer the leafy path that it used to be.

76 For many years there were three classes of travel – first, second and third – which is illustrated by these early tickets. Bicycles could also be taken on the train at a special rate.

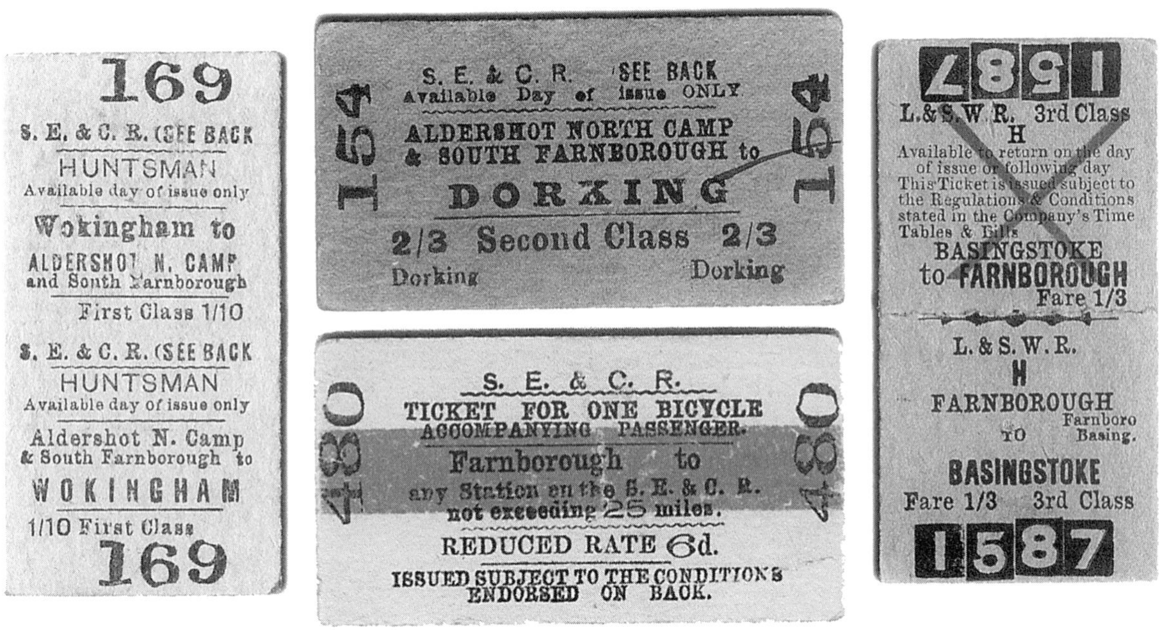

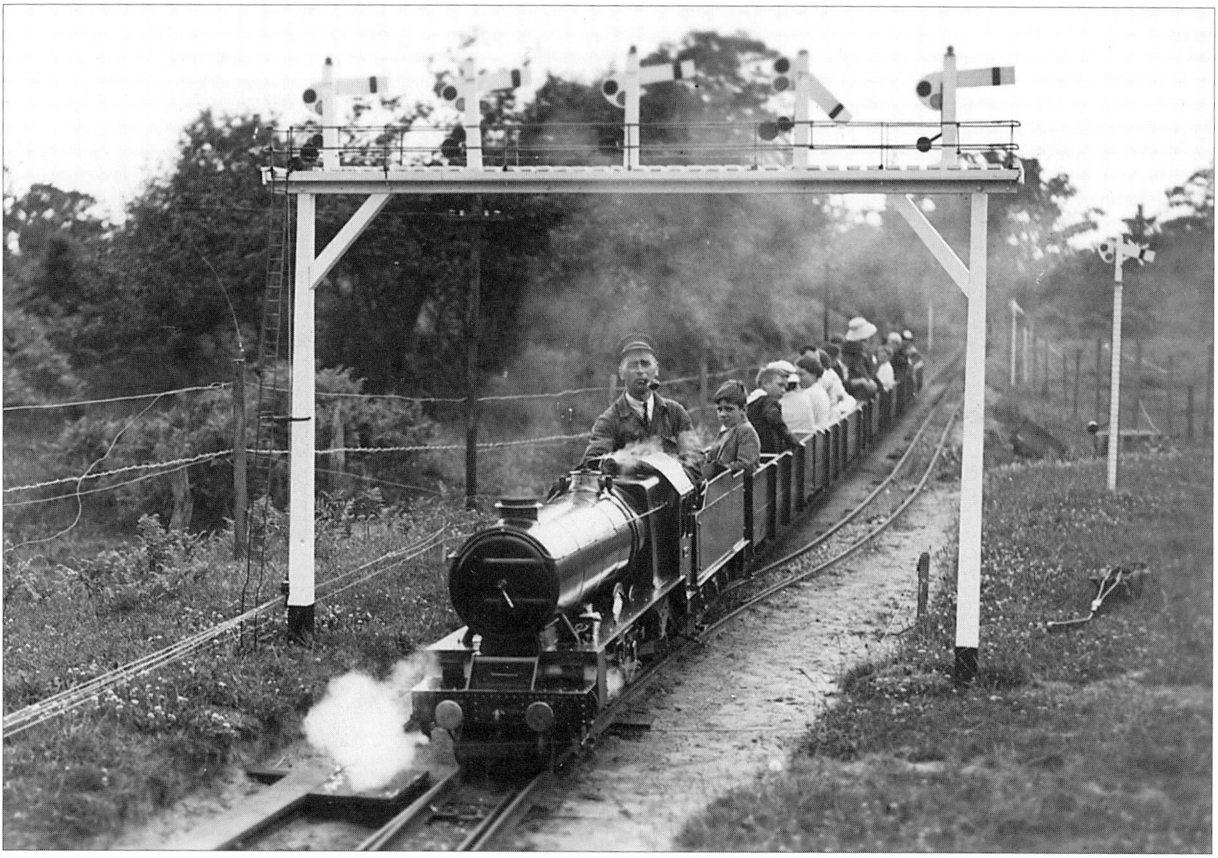

77 Farnborough Miniature Railway, 1937. For a few years, prior to the Second World War, Farnborough had a miniature railway providing enjoyment to many thousands of people. Started by Charles Bullock who lived in Prospect Avenue, it ran through the fields from Foxhill towards Cove Brook in Lye Copse. This engine, driven by Mr Frank, is just approaching Foxhill station.

78 Being tucked away on private farmland, Foxhill was difficult to find, so a larger site for a new miniature railway, to be named the Surrey Borders and Camberley Railway, was found just along the Blackwater River, between the two Southern Electric railway lines. A new station and terminus was built at Farnborough Green just near the junction of Farnborough Road and Hawley Lane. This was easily accessible from the Southern Railway station at Frimley which advertised special excursions to link up with the miniature railway. The miniature railway closed at the onset of war in 1939 and never reopened.

79 The land on which the miniature railway had been built was eventually sold to British Car Auctions whose huge operation filled the whole site. This aerial view shows the Blackwater River meandering through the site, and in the distance the M3, which opened in the early 1970s. British Car Auctions eventually moved to Blackbushe.

80 In 1917 a branch line was built to link the RAE to the mainline station at Farnborough. The lines ran along Elm Grove Road, across Victoria Road and behind the houses into the RAE. The residents of the day were concerned that this railway would be very dangerous, causing damage to property and adversely affecting trade in the shops. Their complaints fell on deaf ears and they were informed that, because it was wartime, this railway was required by the Government in Defence of the Realm but would only be a temporary measure. This train is just entering Elm Grove Road from Victoria Road. Fifty years and another World War passed before the line was closed in 1967. The most famous of the engines was called *Invincible* and today Invincible Road follows the route of the old line.

Six
Motoring Ways

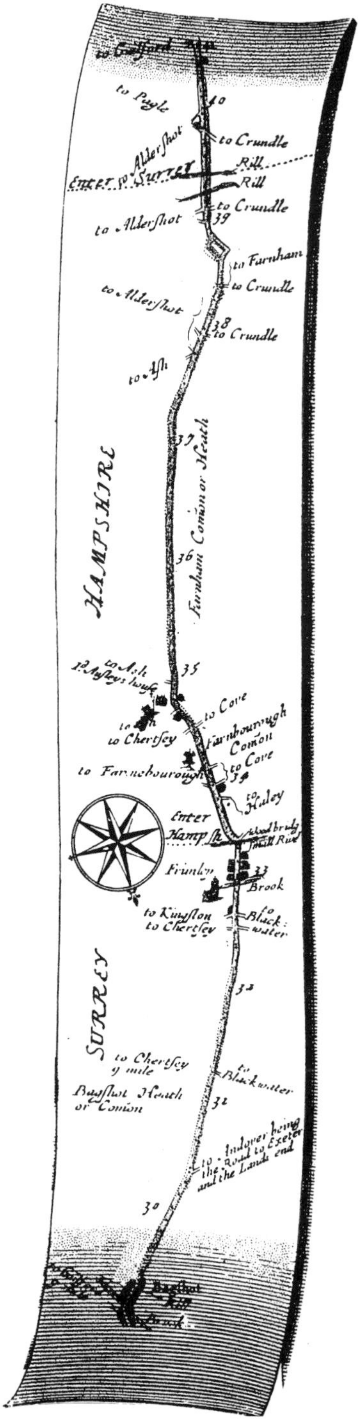

81 Ogilby's Road Map, 1675. In 1666, during the Great Fire of London, John Ogilby, an ex soldier, publisher and favoured poet to Charles II, lost his fortune which was tied up in his home, extensive book collection and shop. Being left virtually penniless, he sought employment in establishing the boundaries of properties lost in the fire. Together with a number of surveyors he produced an outstanding map of the city of London. In 1675, having undertaken a survey of the whole of England, he produced an atlas showing such details as local landmarks, bridges, rivers, fords and hills and whether the roads were enclosed by walls or hedges. The atlas took the form of a series of vertical strips of road and this one of Farnborough shows a windmill on Farnborough Hill, Lord Annesly's House (Farnborough Place) near the church, and clearly marks the roads leading east to Chertsey and west to Cove.

82 Beeching's Garage near The Rex Cinema, 1950s. This garage was originally a coachbuilders established by the Joyce family in the 1860s. Over the years it adapted to the changing methods of transport and from around 1900 started to sell cars. Beeching's had a number of garages including one near the *Queen's Hotel*.

83 From the time that the *Queen's Hotel* was built in 1855, there had been a cabstand or taxi rank on the opposite side of Lynchford Road. Originally, Lynchford Road led from the Farnborough Road through to Ash and in the late 1800s there was a horse-drawn tram which ran on rails taking it from Farnborough station to North Camp station. The through-road is now dual carriageway at this point, leaving the original road as an access to the hotel, which now goes under the corporate name of *Holiday Inn*. In this photograph, taken in the early 1920s, Mr Charles Snare is seen in his own taxi waiting for a passenger. Just beyond the vehicle is a small hut, long since disappeared, giving the telephone number to ring if a taxi was required.

84 In 1935 there were still a number of cesspits in the town and the Council had to empty them. Mr Joe Oliver, who worked for the Council for over 40 years, drove this lorry which could also have a snow plough fitted during the winter months.

85 Bradford's Garage, 1937. On the A325, near the Farnborough Gate shopping area, is Bradford's Roundabout which takes its name from a former garage next to *The Ship Inn*. In 1937, Mr Bradford, who was well established in a part of the town known then as Farnborough Green, decorated his premises for the coronation of King George VI. Being in a prime position as the first garage on the northern approach to the town, the business rapidly expanded from one fuel pump in 1937 to seven pumps in the late 1940s.

86 This view of Bradford's garage, *c*.1950, shows the expansion of the workshops on the right, indicating an increase in servicing as the motor car became more affordable. The garage was also an agency for the Express bus to London and tickets could be purchased in advance from there. Nowadays, under different owners, the site is a modern service station fronting a very busy dual carriageway.

87 Immediately behind Bradford's garage were pits from which gravel was dug for roads during the latter half of the 19th century. When extraction had finished, the land was filled and the RAE Sports and Social Club moved here from their old ground adjacent to the RAE. In the distance, towards Frimley, is a rifle range and some cottages called Spring Villas, all of which have disappeared beneath the Blackwater Valley Relief Road. The bus in the centre is standing on Hawley Lane showing the old position of the road before the roundabout was built.

88 The Cambridge Garage, 1950s. This garage was alongside the old *Cambridge Hotel* on the Farnborough Road, opposite the railway station. The road leading up to the garage is Jubilee Hall Road, named after the Jubilee Hall which stood immediately to the left. The hotel was eventually demolished and a large service station built in its place. That in turn has now been demolished and the whole site is being redeveloped for residential use.

89 F. Knight & Son, 1930s. Fred Knight, who installed one of the first petrol pumps in South Farnborough, is seen here in Cross Street putting petrol into a customer's Norton motor bike. This early petrol pump needed two people to work it. The mechanic on the left is priming the pump ready for use. Subsequently the garage became Jet Service Station but has now been redeveloped as residential homes.

TELEPHONE - - - SOUTH FARNBOROUGH, 107
THE PALACE GARAGE SERVICE
Motor Coaches, Cars and Taxis for Hire
REASONABLE CHARGES & PROMPT ATTENTION
AGENTS for the CUBITT CAR
Any Make of Car Supplied
Easy Payments Arranged
STORAGE FOR 20 CARS
Driving taught. A.A. and M.U. Insurance Agents
Michelin and Dunlop Stockists
THE PALACE GARAGE, CAMP ROAD FARNBOROUGH
PROPRIETORS - - R. FORT & G. NANSON

90 When this advert appeared in a local guide in 1923, Messrs Fort and Nanson's Palace Garage in Camp Road had become a thriving business. Proximity to the large military presence in the North Camp is reflected in the diversity of the services offered. As the motor car became more affordable, the officers and prosperous traders of North Camp were probably in a better position than most to own this more convenient form of transport.

91 In 1937 The Palace Garage, which had become the official Ford dealer in Farnborough, featured in *The Advertiser*, a local 'freebie' newspaper issued by the Farnborough Chamber of Commerce. By then Mr N. S. Barton was the Managing Director of what had become the Palace Garage and Engineering Company Ltd. He is third from the left in this photograph of the staff outside their works and showroom.

92 Mr W.H.T. Cunnington (centre), Chairman of Farnborough Urban District Council, is taking delivery of his new Ford Ten motor car from Mr Barton (right) outside the Town Hall in 1937.

93 After years of austerity throughout the 1940s, people began to look forward to a brighter future, particularly following the coronation of Queen Elizabeth II in 1953. Weddings have always been an expensive occasion and probably this one was no exception in the mid-1950s. George Smith on the left, his sister Rose (centre) and Joe Gainer on the right are waiting for the guests outside St Peter's parish church. Today, one of those number plates alone would probably fetch more than the cost of that wedding.

94 In June 1969 the St John Ambulance Divisions of Farnborough and Cove assembled at their headquarters in Somerset Road for the dedication of their new ambulance. The £2,000 for the ambulance was raised from an appeal launched by the Chairman of Farnborough Council, Mr John Debenham, and was achieved in only 15 months. Such was the generosity of the public that there was sufficient money to complete the new headquarters building on the site.

95 This lorry belonged to J.T. Gaines and Son, builders, and is seen here in Yeovil Road in 1954. Ron Dewing is standing by the cab and John Walker is on the back. They are parked outside Rose Cottage which bears the date plaque of 1870.

96 North Camp Service Station was at the far end of Lynchford Road near North Camp station. This little block of five shops was built in the 1930s and the service station was added in the 1950s by Captain Rees who ran the business with his son Mervyn. Eventually the whole block was demolished and a modern garage replaced the service station. That subsequently closed and the site has now been redeveloped.

97 West Heath Bridge in 1962 when it was closed to all road traffic for six weeks while it was being repaired. This picture was taken before the new bridge had been built alongside. Here, passengers were dropped off at temporary bus stops on either side of the bridge. They then walked through to pick up another bus to continue their journeys.

Seven

Taking to the Air

98 Some of the early balloons outside the western end of the first airship shed, *c.*1910. The huge doors were 72 feet high and were the largest in the country at that time. This was where the army's first airship, *Nulli Secundus*, was constructed in 1907. The men on the right are standing beneath the shadow of the original balloon shed relocated from Aldershot.

99 An army balloon being inflated by a unit of the Army Balloon Section. In the centre of the group sitting on a gas cylinder is Tom Raison Ashdown. The balloons were made of 'goldbeater's skin' derived from the gut of an ox. These skins were purchased from local abattoirs, then cleaned and treated by local women in a workshop in South Farnborough owned by the Weinling family.

100 The airship sheds in 1912. On the right is the skeleton of the portable airship shed structure which was taken down many years ago. It is hoped that it will be re-used in the redevelopment of the historic quarter of the former factory site.

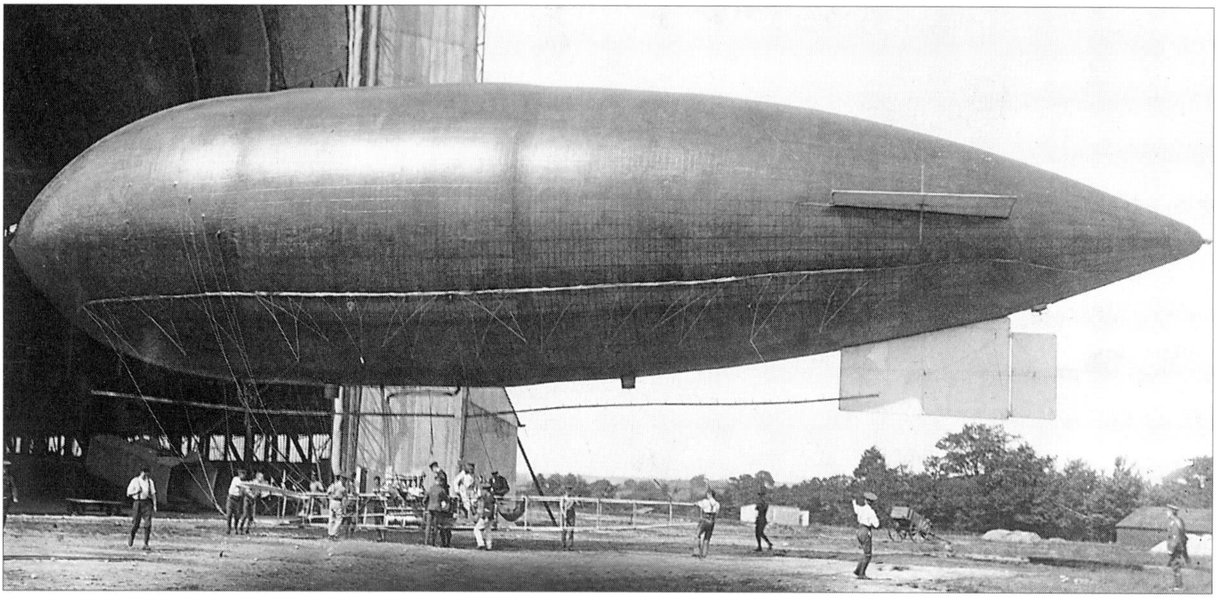

101 The airship *Beta* was originally designed as a smaller experimental craft called *Baby* which took to the air in 1909. *Baby* was very short and dumpy, difficult to steer and rather unstable. After various modifications and ultimate lengthening, it was renamed *Beta* and became one of the most successful army airships of the time. The two bands around the centre part are where the new piece of goldbeater's skin has been inserted to extend the airship out of *Baby*. This postcard of the *Beta* is dated 20 June 1913 and the message on the reverse refers to the excitement of seeing the airship flying over the military tattoo held the previous night at Government House.

102 The *Astra Torres* naval airship was being tested in June 1913. By this time, these craft were much more stable and easier to manoeuvre, thus making them more effective as fighting air machines. With enlarged crew accommodation in the car which hung beneath, it could carry much heavier equipment than the aeroplane which was still in its early stages of development. Innovative equipment such as wireless telegraph to communicate with the ground and telephone equipment for communication between the crew and pilot were also on board. During its trials it suffered a minor leakage which gave rise to this unusual appearance.

103 The first officially recorded powered aeroplane flight in Great Britain was made in 1908 by Samuel Franklin Cody. Born in America, he came to England as a Wild West Showman who developed an interest in kite flying. He was appointed chief instructor of kiting at the Balloon School and helped to develop manned flight. Cody is seen here in 1911 in Army Aeroplane No 1, sometimes referred to as the Flying Cathedral.

104 Michelin Trophy, 1910. Cody's work was often blighted by the scepticism of officialdom concerning the potential use of aeroplanes. The government generally favoured the development of airships. Personal financial difficulties also caused him to turn to the aeronautic show scene to fund his experiments. He entered competitions and in 1910 won the Michelin Trophy after achieving a flight of 17 circuits totalling 189 miles around Laffans Plain; he had been in the air for nearly four-and-a-half hours.

105 Cody's achievements and failures were a constant source of interest to local people but the national press reporting was at times as negative as it is today. One exception that received great accolades in the medical press was his conversion of an aeroplane into an air ambulance. He is seen here accompanied by three passengers and a portable operating table strapped to the side, proving that a three-man medical team could be transported speedily to wherever it was required.

106 The ensuing demonstration illustrated how the operating table could be converted into a stretcher. This concept of the air ambulance was set before the General Medical Council and given an enthusiastic write-up in the *British Medical Journal*. It was eventually recommended for use by the medical wing of the War Office.

107 The ultimate challenge was to fly across the Atlantic so Cody set about designing his entry. By the standards of the day it was huge, having a wingspan of over 60 feet. Cody designed some floats so that it could land on water and he is seen here in 1913 testing it on the Basingstoke Canal. Later that year, Cody's luck ran out and he died when the aeroplane he was flying crashed into a clump of oak trees on Ball Hill at the far end of the airfield.

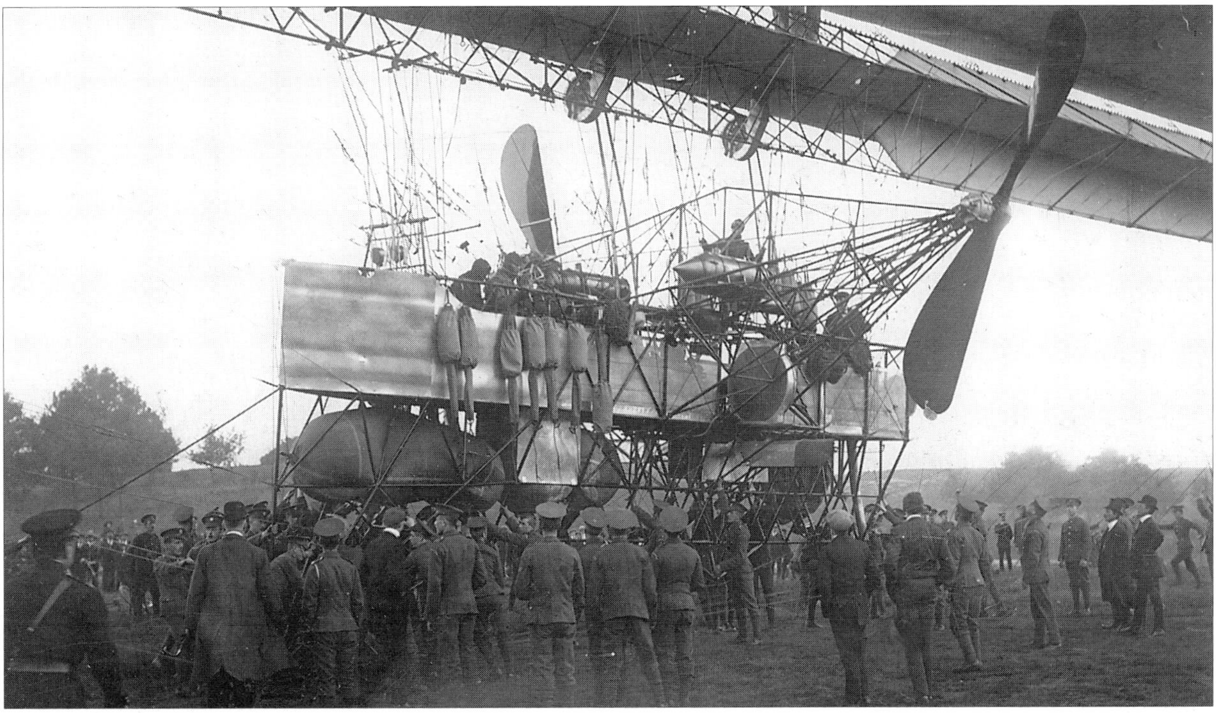

108 The Lebaudy airship was purchased with public contributions arranged by *The Morning Post* newspaper. Built in France with a length of 337 feet, it was larger than any British airship and had flown to Farnborough for trials before being given to the Army Air Corps. The passengers who travelled in the car, which hung beneath the airship, included the commandant of the Balloon School, the French designer, the pilot, three journalists and three mechanics. On being towed into the specially constructed shed, it snagged the roof and collapsed to the ground.

109 The damaged airship was returned to France to be rebuilt and a year later it again made the journey across the channel. Arriving on a windy day, the airship dragged its mooring ropes and drifted across the Farnborough Road, crashing into the garden of Woodlands Cottage, on the corner of Reading Road. A crowd soon gathered to view the wreckage and, according to the local press, to pick up bits and pieces as mementoes of the event.

110 As can be seen, the wreckage was wrapped around a chimney and some trees, but fortunately nobody was hurt and the bulk of the damage was done to the garden. It took two days to clear the site of all the debris which was taken back to the Aircraft Factory. The Lebaudy never flew again. The owner of the house, Colonel Jessop, put in a claim for compensation which was eventually settled but not before a considerable argument with the insurers.

111 In 1911 the Balloon Factory became the Army Aircraft Factory and in 1912 the 'Royal' prefix was added to make the Royal Aircraft Factory. Its remit, laid down by the War Office, was to test British and foreign engines and aircraft, to carry out experimental work, and to train the mechanics of the Royal Flying Corps. That same year these aeroplane sheds were built on Jersey Brow to the west of the site.

112 The royal family had always taken a keen interest in the development of the aeroplane and in May 1914 King George V and Queen Mary visited Farnborough whilst they were staying in Aldershot for a review of the army. The royal couple inspected 27 aircraft and then watched while the planes took off and did a circuit of the airfield. Afterwards, the visitors toured the Factory, finishing with the new Royal Flying Corps barracks being constructed near the Farnborough Road.

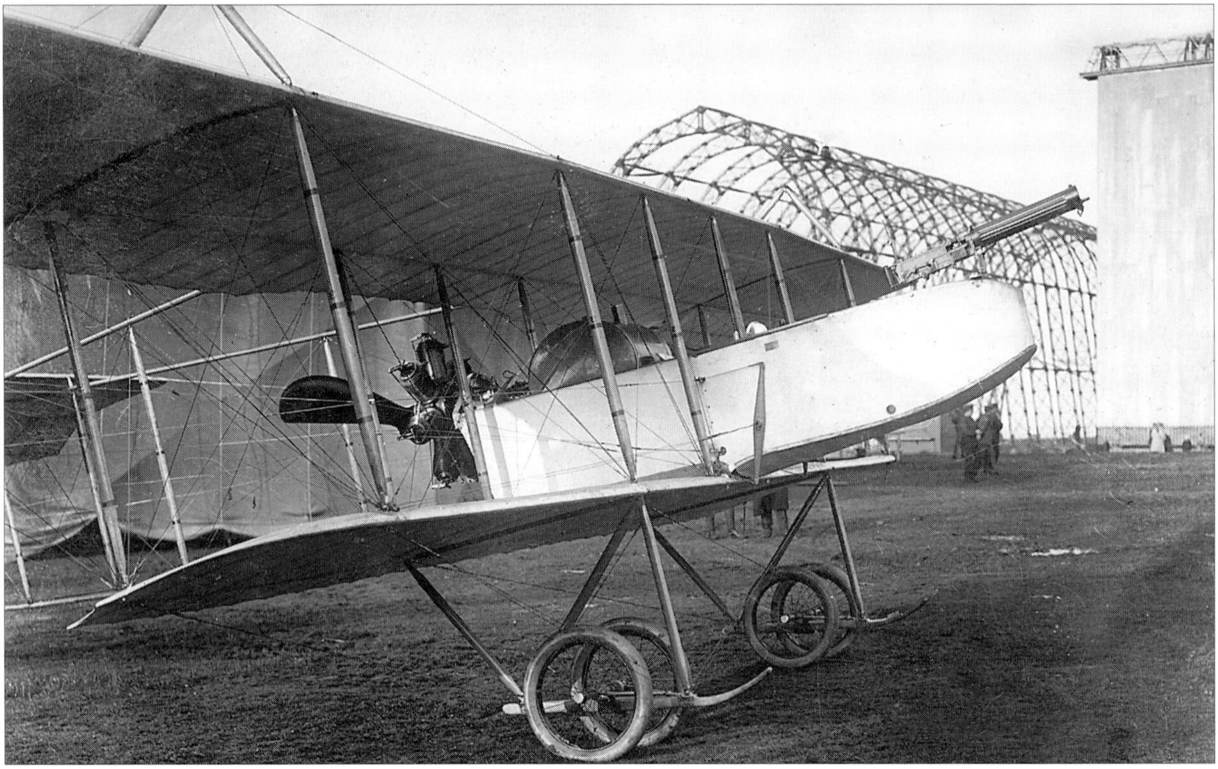

113 This de Havilland FE2, designed and piloted by Geoffrey de Havilland, was one of the first Factory biplanes. With the impending threat of war, it was modified to take a machine gun which could be aimed and operated by a passenger. Initially, it was discovered that the only way the gun could be used effectively was by kneeling or standing up. Further modifications introduced a pivot mounted gun which proved more effective. Geoffrey de Havilland was the Chief Test Pilot at the Factory until 1914.

114 With the onset of the First World War in 1914 there were nearly one thousand people employed at the Factory, which indicates the speed at which the business of research and development was moving forward. Although not intended to be a major manufacturer of aeroplanes, the Factory was allowed vastly to increase its production because the private companies could not cope with the demands of the war. At its height, the workforce expanded to nearly five thousand, many of them local women who are seen here employed in the wood-turning workshop.

115 This was the original Headquarters of the Royal Flying Corps which was established in 1912. The low building on the right was the early Balloon Equipment Store. In 1918 the Royal Flying Corps and the Royal Naval Air Service joined forces to become the Royal Air Force and this became their local Headquarters. The document recording this event was signed by Lord Trenchard in this building. Today known as Trenchard House, it still retains its strong links with early aviation as it is home to the Farnborough Air Sciences Trust and their museum. When the RAF was formed, the old Royal Aircraft Factory changed its name to the Royal Aircraft Establishment in order to avoid confusion over the initials.

RFC
They call us "THE EYES
OF THE ARMY"
For we scout for the foe far and wide,
And with all Information worth having
We keep the powers fully supplied -
There are Corps who bear much longer records
For brave deeds, yet History will find
That in the great fight
for the cause of the right,
OUR AIRMEN were not FAR BEHIND.
FROM ONE OF THE
R.F.C.
FROM FARNBOROUGH.

116 This postcard, issued around 1916, depicts the Royal Flying Corps as the 'Eyes of the Army'.

117 Crested china, *c.*1914. In the early part of the 20th century, as travelling became easier, people wanted to buy souvenirs as mementoes of their visits. Crested china became very popular and, if a place did not have an official crest, then the manufacturers used one from their pattern books. The early Farnborough crest was designed by Mr John Drew, the publisher who had a shop in Lynchford Road. It depicts fern leaves for the old name of Ferneberga, an upturned 'v' representing the ancient tumuli found in the area, local pine trees and the Rose of Hampshire. This aeroplane propeller also featured the crest of the Royal Flying Corps.

118 The Rafborough Estate was constructed during the First World War by prisoners of war for the workers at the Royal Aircraft Factory. Many of the roads were named after former test pilots from the Factory such as Goodden Crescent, Busk Crescent, and Keith Lucas Road, as well as after other personalities, as in Cody Road and Fowler Road. In the foreground can be seen the allotments on the edge of Weir Avenue.

119 This aerial view of the RAE in 1924 shows the extent of its development in just 20 years. In the foreground is the Farnborough Road with the *Swan Inn* to the left. The road beside the *Swan* leads down past the airfield on the left to the airship sheds at the far end. Just beyond them are the RFC aeroplane sheds with Cove Reservoir in the top left-hand corner. On the top right is the Rafborough Estate and centre right are Pinehurst Cottages, also built for RAE workers. The vast majority of the factory buildings have now been demolished but the area to the centre is being redeveloped as the heritage quarter.

120 RAE Inspection Staff, December 1928. Top row, left to right: T.P. Fisk, B.C. Hampton, D.G. Hankins, W. Mitchell, T. Saxby, W.H. Barnes, F. Fossey, H. Almond, E.J. Perrott, T.H. Harcourt, A. Fletcher; second row: A.W. Southerton, G.W. Bailey, S.H. Ratcliff, W.J. Laird, L.E. Jones, C.C. Hoskins, E.H. Holman, R.J. Smith, W.N. Peters, H. Hewitt, J.E. Owen; front row: A.H. Dunster, W.Olsen, F.H. Nailor, J. Salter, C.F. White, F.C.J. Aylesbury, F.R.R. Chapman, C. Harrison, L.J. Wearing.

121 The Pyestock Chimney, late 1920s. This chimney was built around 1900 near Norris Bridge to the north of the Basingstoke Canal. At 140 feet high it was intended to be part of a refuse destructor for the Aldershot Camp but it was never actually used for the purpose and remained a 'white elephant' until its demolition in 1930. It was used for a few years during the First World War as a meteorological observation station when it had a glass dome on top, accessed by an internal ladder.

122 This RAF Meteor Mark 9 from No 2 Squadron was based in Germany on fighter reconnaissance. It carried cameras and recording equipment and came to the RAE at Farnborough for some modifications. Before going back to Germany the pilot had to clear customs but the nearest airfield with these facilities was Blackbushe. The weather conditions were very poor and the aircraft suffered a mishap on landing, which necessitated a further return to Farnborough for repairs. The wings were removed and the remainder of the rather forlorn looking craft was towed back along the A325 Farnborough Road via the Clockhouse in March 1950. In those days the road was quite narrow so the exercise caused considerable disruption to traffic. The Clockhouse looks a little different today as the cupola has since been lowered. The Zebra crossing has also disappeared.

123 Although the number of people employed at the RAE was greatly reduced after the Second World War, in the 1960s it was still the largest employer in the town. At clocking-off time, the workers streamed out onto the Farnborough Road, at this exit beside the *Swan Inn*. In the early days the vast numbers of cyclists pouring out caused considerable chaos in the rush hour. Mr Harry Roberts is the gentleman right at the front of the picture. After working there for 25 years, he received the Imperial Service Medal in 1961.

Eight
Education

124 Farnborough School opened in 1873 in a large house called Castledon Hall which had been built by William Knell, an early land developer. Because of its proximity to the army camp with its huge numbers of military personnel, Farnborough was home to numerous preparatory schools. These schools attained a high degree of excellence and attracted pupils from far and wide as an onward step to such places as Harrow, Eton and Dartmouth. In this photograph taken in 1912, the joint Headmasters are in the second row: left to right: D.L. Ingpen, R.B. Whicher, A.C. Connal, E.C. Cumberbatch, V.A.C. Findlay, R.A. Ingram (Head), Mrs E.G. North, E.G.H. North (Head), P. Bloomfield, W.S. Clowes, D.G. Eagar and A.F. Barnes. The school was moved to Sonning just before the Second World War and Castledon Hall was demolished in the 1950s to make way for what is now the Farnborough College of Technology.

125 Still drawing pupils from military families, many of those in this photograph of 1931 went on to high ranking military or diplomatic posts. One former pupil recalls the first verse of the school song which describes perfectly the surrounding area of pines and gorse: ''Mid heather, gorse and broom, 'mid Hampshire fir and pine, There stands the School where I would be: Here's to its flag, the Fleur de Lys, Here's to your school and mine.' In the photograph left to right from the back: J.H. Smith Carrington, D.S. Winckworth, N.W.I. Napier, J.H.D. Richardson, ?, ?, ?, J.F. Lowder, ?, ?, ?, ?, ?, ? Thomas, ?, ?, ?, H.E.W. Arnott, ?, ?, G.F. Bell, ? Ormrod, D.P. Seeley, ?, D.M. Barbour, R.J.M. Harley, G.N.R. Drury-Fuller, P. Lockett, ?, I.D.S. Forbes, ?, A.F. Lamb, K.M. Barbour, A.J. Miller, R.H. Deny, R.J. Beech, A.D. Telfer Smollett, ?, J.W. Poston, M.A. Demetriadi, H.M. Sturges, ?, ?, ?, ?. Front row: N.W.N. Frayling, Assistant Matron, H.E.K. Pembroke, A.N. Selbie, W.S. Clowes (having been on the staff since 1912), C.L. Coles, E.K. Stephenson (Head), ?, L.G. Crawley, ?, Matron, ?, ?, R.B. Whicker, C.J.R. Richards. Ground: ?, ?, D.E. Burnett Stuart, ?, H.A.H. King.

126 From its inception the school excelled at sports. Originally using playing fields on the western side of the Farnborough Road, accessed via a pedestrian tunnel, it sold that land to the Government in 1914. The money was ploughed into even better sports facilities within the school grounds, including squash courts, playing fields, cricket nets, football and cricket pitches and an indoor swimming pool. Carpentry was taught and some of the boys had their own gardening plots. The football team in the photograph of 1932 shows Patrick Lockett as captain in the centre.

127 The Lord Mayor of London, Col. Sir William Dunn, Bart., performed the opening ceremony at a fête and bazaar held in the grounds of Hillside Convent at the top of Star Hill in 1917. Members of Farnborough Council also attended, some of whom are in this photograph: left to right: ?, Chairman of the Council G.W. Collins, JP, The Lady Mayoress (a former pupil at Hillside), The Lord Mayor, Princess Clementine Napoleon, ?, T.J. Wilkes; back row: ?, ?, ?, ?, J. Yeoman, Rev. A. Sutherland. Such a distinguished gathering was brought together to help raise funds for the Red Cross Societies of England and France and nearly all the guests are wearing red cross flags in their lapels. Princess Clementine and her family stayed with the Empress Eugénie at Farnborough Hill for the duration of the First World War as it was safer than living at their home in Belgium. Over £500 was raised at the two-day event, which had attracted hundreds of people, including local traders, who had donated generously towards the stalls and prizes.

128 The Dining Room at Pinewood School. This was originally built by William Knell as a private house in Albert Road. The very large rooms in these old Victorian houses were ideal for conversion into school use, as can be seen here where the room is set up for more than seventy pupils and staff, in the 1930s.

129 The dormitory shows fairly austere conditions; jugs for water, a bowl for washing and chamber pots beneath the table. No bedside lockers or tables for personal items, and very little cupboard space was provided. A strip of carpet and a rug in front of the fireplace seem to be the only concession to comfort.

130 Physical Training was also part of the daily routine, come rain or shine. At one time there was a retired Army Gymnastic Instructor, Mr William Fitch, who used to circulate between Hillside, Farnborough School and Belgrave House to give instruction to the pupils. This photograph at Pinewood also shows the formal tree planting which formed part of the garden of the original house. Later requisioned for accommodation during the Second World War, followed by use as a furniture repository, it was eventually demolished to make way for houses.

131 Farnborough Secondary School play entitled 'Le Trésor de Carnac', presented in French at their speech day in 1929. Farnborough Secondary School started life as Farnborough Junior Technical School for boys in 1922 occupying some wooden buildings next to the grounds of the RAE. In 1925 the education system was reorganised and the following year the Technical School converted to a mixed Secondary School and moved across the road into buildings that were formerly occupied by St Mary's Convent. Mr R.H. May was the headmaster.

132 The number of pupils attending the school rapidly increased and it was soon grossly overcrowded. By 1936, the new Grammar School for boys was built in Prospect Avenue so the boys transferred there and the girls went to Aldershot High School. Most of the staff transferred to one or other of the schools, although Mr May took another headship in the New Forest. The teaching staff of 1934-35 in the photograph are: back row, left to right: Messrs Williams, Smith, Murton, James, Mills, Openshaw, Lees; front row: The Misses Martin, Clarke, Jones, Messrs May, Gallemore, the Misses Dean and Collins.

133 There were numerous small private schools in the town and this is the Wellingtonia in Salisbury Road in 1930. In the photograph, back row left to right: Gwen Harris, Peter Wilson, Brian Dungay, Patrick Harris, Peter Greenwood, ?, ?; middle row: ?, ?, Freda Lockspier, ?, Ruth Lineham, ?; front row: ?, Mary Davis, Daphne Hazel, Annie Mardles, Joyce Barber.

134 Mrs E. Pearce was the first Head Mistress to hold office in the Farnborough District, receiving her appointment at the Wesleyan Schools in Lynchford Road in 1881. She was then appointed Head of the infants at the Queen's Road Schools in 1912. When she retired in 1917, she had achieved the maximum of 45 years' service as a teacher. During her 36 years in Farnborough she had taught more than four thousand children. Her achievement even won the approval of the King who, through the Prime Minister's office, sent his congratulations.

135 Queen's Road School football team, 1949. The Headmaster, Mr Charlton, is standing back row left with Mr Payne on the right. Second row fourth from left is Dennis Fisher. Front row from the left: ? Walker, ?, A. Worgan, John Charlton, ?. A team was always entered in the local Junior League and many cups were competed for within the school. Sports activities took place in the Queen's Road Recreation Ground until 1959 when the facilities at the Technical College in Boundary Road began to be used. In 1956 the school became South Farnborough Junior School, admitting pupils up to the age of 11 only and today it is South Farnborough Infants School; the older pupils attend the Junior School at Cunnington Road.

136 In 1949 the school choir entered the Aldershot Festival of Music and Drama which was held in the Grosvenor Road Methodist Church. All the entries were of a very high standard and the competition was keen from schools throughout the area. Queen's Road School was beaten into second place by Onslow County Secondary School near Guildford. Left to right, back row: David Bury, Stewart McAngus, David Anderson, ?, Denis Fisher, Craig Vincent, ?, Ray Clubs, Robin Levitt; next: Mr Charlton (Head), Sheila Foster, Maureen Finch, Avril Hoare, Olive Lambert, Margaret Milne, Connie Overton, ?, Jean Wakefield, ?, Jean Finn, Dawn Bowyer, Catriona Rowsel, Mr Trill (music teacher); next: Sylvia Gordon, Judy Taylor, Leonie Churn, Betty Beasley, ?, Hetty Alison, Veronica Latham, Daphne Doe, Pat Masterson, Jean Andrews, Susan Glasscock, Joan ?, Jennifer Green; next: Anne Dowrick, Jennifer Jeremy, Margaret Watts, Trish Shelley, Valerie Taylor, Pat Senior, ?, Joey Gibson, Pauline Wareham, Eve Thorn, Pat Pancott; front: Alan Bailey, Terry New, Andrew Blair, Tony Garrett, Albert Ives.

137 Aerial view of South Farnborough Junior School and surroundings in 1970. The school is centre right with the catholic church of Our Lady Help of Christians next door, adjacent to the three-storey building which was part of the Salesian College. A new church now stands on the corner site but the remainder of the college grounds and premises can be seen top left.

138 Salesian College Form VI, 1950. Left to right, standing: R.R. Carter, P. Hicks, K. Keegan, G. Goodridge; seated: G. Popley, B. Mason, H. Davis, Fr C. Murphy, P. Wilson, J. Dolan, C. Poffley. The Salesian fathers came to Farnborough in 1901 and took over an orphanage which was housed in the former tin factory on the corner of Queen's and Sherborne Roads. It soon became a regular boarding school for boys and in 1912 it was extended along Sherborne Road. Further expansion in Reading Road provides facilities for this Independent Catholic Grammar School for boys aged 11 to 18 years.

139 The Wavell School was built in 1970 by the Hampshire Education Authority for children of army families on land made available by the Ministry of Defence. Taking in around 450 pupils from the age of 11 to 15, it also drew in children from the families of RAE workers and the local civilian population. Situated on Lynchford Road, near the old *Queen's Hotel*, the site was formerly old army barracks in North Camp. When it opened it had the benefit of a larger than average amount of tarmac surface for play areas which was a relic of its former use, as can be seen from this aerial view taken in 1970. The school was named after Field Marshal Earl Wavell, General Officer Commanding in Chief, Southern Command, in 1938-39 and whose family had long military associations with the area. Today it has around 800 pupils but, because of the reduction in military personnel in the area, only about 25 per cent come from military families.

Nine
Social Scenes

140 In 1861, the Aldershot Camp Races took place on the Queen's Parade in North Camp. The course was set out along the northern bank of the Basingstoke Canal, turned northwards parallel to the Farnborough Road, with the finishing line and Grandstand in front of the *Queen's Hotel*. This popular event drew crowds of spectators who arrived in their carriages, causing chaotic scenes on the roads nearby. Many stalls and booths were set up to sell their wares and entertain the visitors. The newspapers of the day reported that the lively scene was one to rival the races at Epsom with its colourful military and civilian presence, enhanced by the numerous ladies representing the beauty and fashion of the neighbourhood! This cup to the value of 100 guineas was presented by the Farnborough tradespeople who, no doubt, welcomed this influx of wealthy visitors.

141 The volunteer service women from the Ladies Auxiliary formed themselves into a hockey club and in 1922, captained by Miss Manning, they had an excellent season, losing only one match. Their success was attributed to the fact that they often played against men's teams drawn from other branches of the Services. In the photograph, taken in the grounds of Belgrave House School, are Miss Jean Haliday (goal-keeper), Miss Rene Westcott (vice captain), Mrs Lees, Mrs Wheland, the Misses Biddy and Leila Manning, Miss Gleaker, Mrs Collins, Miss Chipperton, Miss Betty Watkins, Miss Dora Wiles and Miss Connie Dacombe.

142 Great interest was generated when in 1922 the local constabulary challenged the Council to a cricket match. The Police won by 47 runs and the crowd that gathered in Queen's Road Recreation ground to watch was quite pleased that the local council had taken a beating. In the photograph are: back row, left to right: Council Chairman, G.W. Collins, Col. H.E. Pennethorne, P.F. Allen, E.H.G. North (Council), Supt. W. Davies, PC's Stone, Cooper, Passingham, PS Marshall, PC's Dolby and Horn. Front row: Dr E. Croft-Watts, L. Coleman, A.G. Chambers, J. Yeoman, F.C. Sandberg JP (Council), PS Hobbs, PS Payne, PC Savage, PS Bunning and, in the front, PC Wagstaff.

143 Cove Reservoir, *c.*1930. This was a popular recreational facility which had been constructed by the army in 1861 to train horses to cross deep water, as a watering place for the horses, and a bathing place for the troops. Some trees were planted to give shade to the bathers. The *Aldershot Military Gazette* reported in 1861 that the cost of around £1,000 could be justified as it had to pay £20 per month for each cavalry regiment making use of the nearby Basingstoke Canal for watering the horses. Allegedly, a Saxon spearhead was dug up but there is no official record of such a find, although the newspaper reported that one of the captains had taken charge of it. The Reservoir was recognised by the Council as one of the local facilities until the Second World War when it was drained, like many ponds, to eliminate any possible landmarks from the eyes of the enemy.

144 A parade of the Ancient Order of Foresters going down the road from the *Swan* to the RAE for a meeting on the aerodrome in the late 1930s. Front row, left to right: Mrs Andrewartha, Gus Bartlett, Miss Bartlett and Jack Morrish; next row: Ralph Woods, Cecil Gosney, with R. (Bob) Allum behind and Mrs Woods behind him. Mrs Jarvis is behind Mr Morrish with Mr Tulip behind him.

145 During the first Farnborough Carnival in 1934, more than one hundred decorated vehicles took part in the procession which was over a mile long. The winner of the Tableau Cars section was the entry by the Ancient Order of Foresters, North Farnborough branch, depicting Robin Hood and his Merry Men in a woodland setting. This photograph was taken in Farnborough Street before the float set off to join the parade.

146 There were dozens of other different events at the Carnival including Indoor Cycling in the Town Hall, a Masked Ball, Whist Drive and a Baby Show at which there were more than one thousand entries. More than five hundred children took part in the children's fancy dress procession which commenced on Cove Green and marched through Farnborough to the Fair Ground where the participants all had free rides at the fair. Winners of the Hired Costume Group were Bride and Bridegroom Sheila Challis and Peter Machin.

147 The coronation of King George VI took place in 1937 and one of the main celebrations in Farnborough was a huge ox roast held in Queen's Road Recreation Ground. It took eight cwt of coal and six cwt of wood to roast the huge beast which had been donated by Mr A. Hewett, seen here in the centre wearing a bowler hat. Cooking went on from 9 a.m. until the first cut was made at 4 p.m. The 'cook' was Mr Fred Tyler from Stratford on Avon, who was an expert at such roasts, and the local boy scouts helped with the basting and turning. Seventy-five large loaves were cut up for the hot beef sandwiches which were sold in aid of the coronation fund.

148 No. 2 Platoon, A Company of the 25th Hampshire Regiment Home Guard in 1940 on parade in Boundary Road. Formerly they were known as Local Defence Volunteers. Back row: left, J. G. Hopton, Tony Lax in front; front row: F. Stringer with Bob Allum next; out front: S. Weller and P.R.T. Instone. This platoon numbered around 150 local men who were generally in full-time work and spent all of their spare time 'doing their bit' for the war effort. There were some strategic points locally which needed guarding, mostly along the main railway line to Waterloo. Two of the more regular patrol areas were the concrete 'pill-box' by the Prospect Road Bridge and the bridge by Farnborough railway station. The men also did guard duties at the local telephone exchange and the post office.

149 Girls Training Corps, 1944. The local branch of the Girls Training Corps was based at Queen's Road Council School and flourished until a few years after the Second World War. Its membership was made up of girls from across the town and began as a spin-off from the 14/20 Youth Club also based at the school. They learned about service and community life from lectures and practical demonstrations which provided a good basis for those who wished to go into the Services. Among those on parade are Margaret Cox, Sylvia Watts, Rose Roberts and Brenda Young. One of the officers was Madeleine Poulter.

150 There were joyous celebrations when the Second World War ended in Europe in May 1945. Many parties were held across the town, in public recreation areas, on roads, and in gardens, like this one in the grounds of Abbotsleigh on the corner of Canterbury and Church Roads for the residents of Woodland Grove. It may not have been a very warm day but the children certainly seem to be enjoying themselves, tucking in to the cakes and sandwiches which miraculously appeared despite all the food shortages. Among the children in the photograph are Chris Farr, immediately above the urn which is perched precariously on one of the wooden benches, and David Lelliott, at the end of the table turning round to look at the camera. Abbotsleigh has now been demolished and Woodlands Grove is now named The Grove.

151 Many companies took their workers and families on annual outings and in the early 1950s Mr Jim Gaines (snr) is seen here in front of the Comfy Coach hired from Farnham. At one time Mr Gaines employed more than 20 men in his building business but, after the Second World War, building licences were restricted because of the shortage of materials, so the company had to downsize. The photograph, taken in front of houses in Yeovil Road, also shows early television aerials which began to appear as television became more affordable.

152 The Enthusiasts Club was a youth club started by a group of enthusiastic youngsters in 1951. Run entirely by people under the age of 21, within nine months it had 70 members. It was a very structured club with an organising committee offering a varied programme of activities to suit all tastes, including swimming, cycling, rambling, model engineering, debating, photography and music. Their first President was Brian Mason and some of the early leaders were Hugh Davies (at whose parents' home in Sycamore Road the initial meetings were held), Peter Hicks, John Cushine, David Lloyd and Peter Weare. Social events were popular and this photograph shows their fancy dress social held at St Albans Hall in December 1952. Left to right, back row: Corianne Power, John Cushine, Robert Nash, Peter Hicks, Margaret Rees, Miriam Hearne, Hugh Davies, Michael McGurgan, Eileen Knobbs, ?, Margaret Gemmell, P. Rowe; middle row: Michael Fletcher, Peter Weare, Shirley Gillard, Eileen Eltringham, Beryl Faint, Beryl Machin, Beryl Wollen, Joan Guy, Brian Guy, John Wilding; front row: Maureen O'Bryan, Valerie Watkins, Brenda Curtis, June Curtis, Shirley Hicks, Jeanette Hicks, Jacqueline Hunt, Yvonne Vivian, Eileen Cheeseworth, Graham Edwards, Brian Ruffle, Peter Wilding.

153 At a local fête, the Club had a tent in which they put on an exhibition of the club activities. On the printing section stand are, left to right: Peter Turner, Peter Inglis, Jimmy Gaines (almost hidden), John Penn (wearing a cap), Carl Inglis, Eileen Knobbs, Patrick Garton and Jeffrey Arm. Michael Hall is in the front. The club survived for a few years but membership gradually waned. Today there is a thriving Railway Enthusiasts Club, whose founders were some of the former members of the Enthusiasts Club who had a passion for railways.

154 Farnborough's first students' rag day was organised by the RAE Technical College in September 1952. Several hundred students subjected the town to a variety of practical jokes and youthful exploits, like painting giant footprints everywhere, playing human chess with shoppers, picnicking in the road to stop the traffic and other good-natured antics. The streets of South Farnborough were decorated with streamers and there was a large procession of floats. The success of the event encouraged the students to make it an annual affair along the lines of the student rags which were normally associated with the universities. Many of the traders generously supported the students and, despite the temporary disruption to traffic, welcomed the procession as it brought out huge crowds along the route, as seen here in Camp Road in 1955.

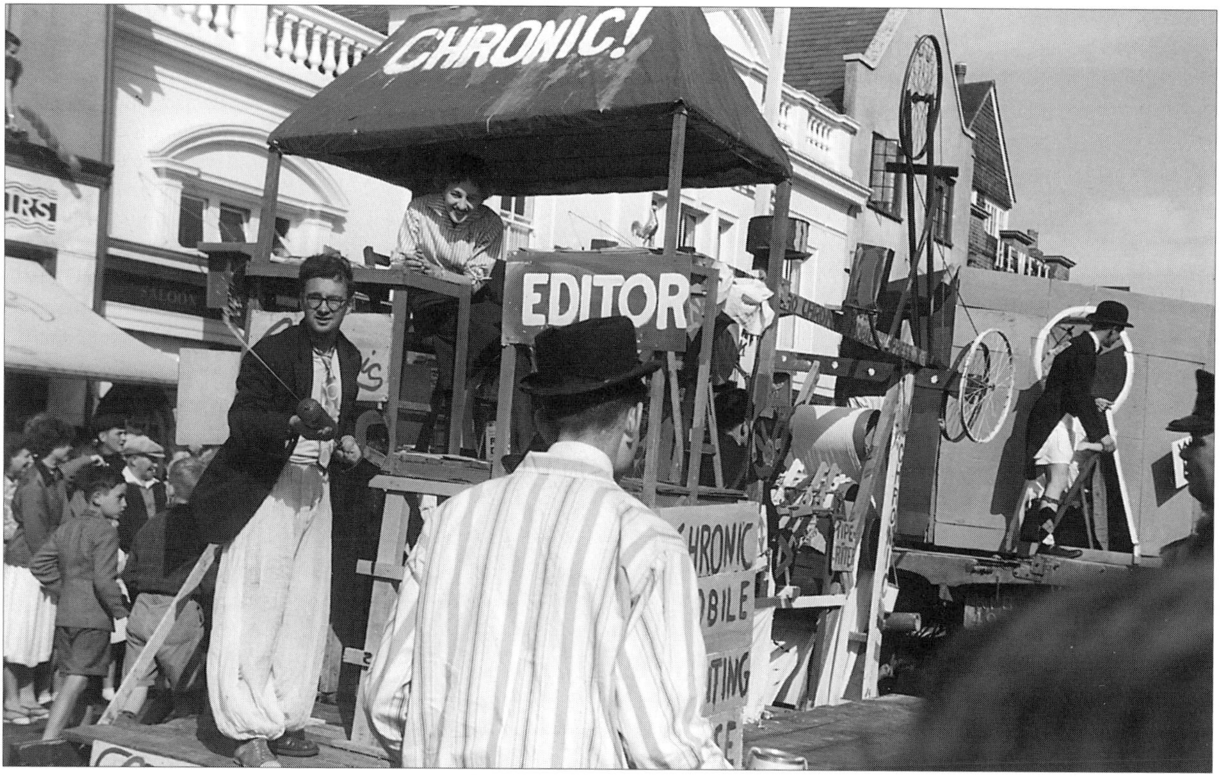

155 By 1955 the rag weeks were well established. The rag newspaper, *The Chronic*, was usually a sell-out and helped to boost the funds raised for charity. Here, in the procession, 'The Chronic' float is depicting a giant printing press powered by bicycle wheels. What the bowler-hatted gentleman can see through the keyhole behind it is left to the imagination. To this day, the former RAE Apprentices' Association still have their newsletter which they call *The Chronic*. Close association with the various RAE departments proved very useful when it came to finding suitable materials for the floats. These were constructed by the students themselves at the RAE Apprentices Hostel, opposite the *Queen's Hotel*, which was the starting point for the procession.

156 The Tramps' Tea party, held on the pavement outside the Scala cinema in Camp Road, was obviously a very casual affair, and their drinking habits in public would certainly contravene the local bylaws of today. However, it was all done in the name of charity to the bemusement of the young spectators on the left.

157 The Rag Queen for 1955 was Pat Gates who led the procession through Farnborough and Cove in an open sports car. Another of her duties was to open the Fair run by Mr George Smitham on Cove Green. She and her attendants, Joan Baker and Jillian Sorton, arrived by helicopter after a short trip from the airfield.

158 The finale of the week was the annual Rag Ball held in the RAE Assembly Hall where more than 600 students danced to the music of Nat Temple and his band. Among the guests was Humphrey Lestocq, a popular BBC personality of the day. Rag Queen Pat, flanked by her attendants, is seen here greeting the principal of the RAE Technical College, Mr R.D. Peggs, and his wife. After a few successful years the annual antics of the students during rag weeks became rather over exuberant and the novelty began to wear off, resulting in less enthusiastic support from the public.

159 Farnborough Street Methodist Church Sunday School Anniversary in 1957. Among those in this photograph are: Rosalie Hastings, Evelyn Durrett, Helen Clifford, Bill Gosney, Carol Norbron, May Pusey, Jack Shepherd, Win Miles, Griff Richards, Hazel Goddard, Eileen Bennett, John Lewis and Kitty Gosney. The line up is in Farnborough Street, outside the Methodist Church, and in the distance are the old buildings of North Farnborough station with the signal box adjacent to the crossing gates.

Ten

Flight to Fame

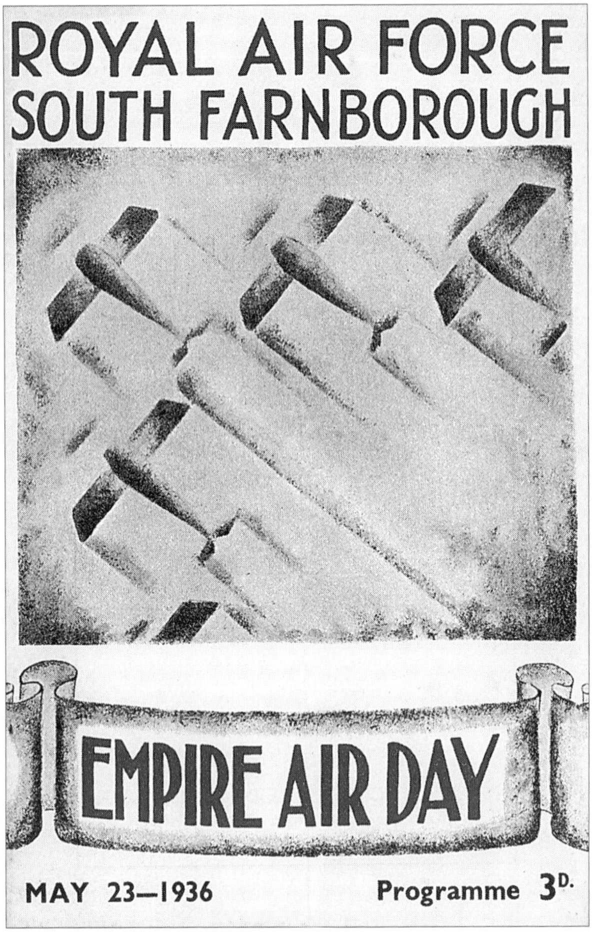

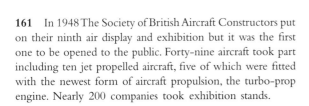

160 The Royal Air Force Station at Farnborough put on a display for Empire Day in 1936. The purpose of such displays was to give the public the opportunity of seeing the normal life and working conditions within the Service. A large crowd was able to enjoy a display of aerobatics, dive bombing, formation flying and other aerial demonstrations, as well as visiting the workshops and exhibits. There were a number of units based at Farnborough Aerodrome, the oldest being No 4 (Army Co-operation) Squadron which formed in 1912 as part of the Royal Flying Corps.

161 In 1948 The Society of British Aircraft Constructors put on their ninth air display and exhibition but it was the first one to be opened to the public. Forty-nine aircraft took part including ten jet propelled aircraft, five of which were fitted with the newest form of aircraft propulsion, the turbo-prop engine. Nearly 200 companies took exhibition stands.

162 Thousands of people attended the show. Special trains were put on and the Aldershot & District Traction Company ran dozens of extra buses to transport passengers from the railway stations. All those visitors required feeding and there were eight large catering points set up. Here in one of the decorated sheds the tables are laid up for a formal lunch. The menu obviously included one bottle of Simonds beer per person but there only seems to be one bottle of wine on each table. Simonds was a brewery based in Reading but it had a large bottling plant in North Farnborough.

163 So large and important was the Farnborough Air Show that the trade visitors were offered every facility to carry out their business. There were no mobile telephones in those days but there was a dedicated Air Show telephone exchange. A mobile Post Office was also brought on to the site and used its own special handstamp, as illustrated on this registered letter posted at the Air Show in 1952.

G-APEV

G-AKTW
WESTLAND
Widgeon

164-166 These three aircraft were among over 170 on display at the 1957 Air Show.

167 King Leopold of the Belgians, in the dark glasses, together with Lord Louis Mountbatten on the left are inspecting a new research Vertical Take Off and Landing Aircraft at the 1958 Air Show.

SOUTHERN

Society of British Aircraft Constructors

FLYING DISPLAY and EXHIBITION

at

Farnborough

FRIDAY, SATURDAY & SUNDAY
SEPTEMBER 7th, 8th & 9th

COMBINED

RAIL & ROAD CHEAP DAY TICKETS

TO

FARNBOROUGH AIRFIELD

(via ALDERSHOT)

By Trains due destination at or before 3.0 p.m.

→ **RETURN BY ANY TRAIN SAME DAY** ←

Passengers should ascertain if (and where) change of carriage is necessary

The Aldershot and District Traction Company will operate road services between Aldershot Railway Station and the Airfield

In addition to the normal services, a number of special trains will be arranged from Waterloo to Aldershot on each day of the show calling at Surbiton, Walton-on-Thames, Weybridge and Woking. Special return trains will also be run as required.

→ FOR DETAILS OF FARES, SEE OTHER SIDE ←

NOTICE AS TO CONDITIONS—These tickets are issued subject to the British Transport Commission's published Regulations and Conditions applicable to British Railways obtainable free of charge at station booking offices, also to the Published Conditions of the Aldershot and District Traction Co. Ltd.

Waterloo Station S.E.1.
July, 1962

S.W.740/$\frac{A30}{26762}$

Printed in Great Britain by
C.M.D Printers Ltd., London and Chatham

168 Handbill advertising special cheap-day combined rail and road tickets to the Airshow in 1962. The Aldershot & District Traction Company ran a special shuttle service to link up with the trains.

169 The Farnborough Air Show is a shop window for the world to buy and sell aviation products. Not only are aeroplanes on show but also the latest in defence weaponry, as shown in this photograph taken in 1978 of a BAE Hawk. This trainer aircraft had the capability of carrying any one of the rockets on show.

170 The renowned Red Arrows aerobatic team are synonymous with the Farnborough Air Show. Formation flying and aerobatics performed by the RAF have always been a feature and before 1965 such names at the Black Arrows, Blue Diamonds and Yellowjacks were seen. By 1965 the Gnat trainer aircraft of the RAF's official display team had been painted red and the Red Arrows took to the skies. The familiar diamond formation of nine aircraft was introduced in 1968 and is still the classical example of precision flying for which the Red Arrows are famous. The spectacular low-flying formations across the airfield, with red, white and blue smoke trails, are a thrilling part of their display, as seen here in 1978.

171 One of the Red Arrows display team, on the runway ready for take-off.

British

172 Concorde made its debut at Farnborough Air Show in 1970 when it enthralled the crowds with its elegant lines and graceful appearance. Of all the aircraft that have ever flown, this was probably the one which created the most excitement and admiration. By 1978 it was in full commercial service with British Airways but because of its tight schedules there was doubt about its being included in the air display. Nevertheless, at the last moment, British Airways bowed to popular demand, and on the last day of the 1978 Air Show this magnificent achievement in supersonic aviation put in a brief appearance to the delight of the crowds. In 2003 Concorde flew for the last time as it was no longer commercially economic and this brought to an end another glorious chapter in our aviation history.

Bibliography

Books:

Callingham, L.F., and Watson, M., *Cove Old and New*, Wm May & Co, Aldershot
Challacombe, Jessie, *Jottings from a Farnborough Notebook* Gale & Polden
Gosney, Jo, *Farnborough Past*, Phillimore
Mitchell, Peter, Shelmerdine, Malcolm, and Townsend, Simon, *Surrey Border & Camberley Railway* Plateway Press
Mostyn, Dorothy A., *The Story of a House* St Michael's Abbey Press

Archives:

Hampshire Records Office
Surrey Family History Centre

Documents:

Farnborough Enclosure Award 1811

Reports:

Caunter, C.F., *Historical Summary of the Royal Aircraft Establishment* HMSO
Report on Train Accident 1947 published by HMSO
Illustrated London News

Newspaper publications:

Aldershot News
Farnborough Advertiser
Sheldrake's Military Gazette

Index

AUTOGRAPHS

J. R. Murphy
Sarnia + Detroit

Hookle J. J.
129 Finkle St.
Woodstock, Ont.

Harry B. Sgt
London Ontario

Reg Kirby

A. W. Waite Chatham

G. W. Drover

Earl R. Pannabecker

M. Robinson London Ont

S. Ahman

F. Bachynski

W. A. Bymewrit

Jas. H. Dakin

R. E. Zugnel Provost

R. J. Lesperance
Windsor Ont.

R. E. Batting

I. L. Pennington
Chatham

R. J. Dianes

L. A. Basson

Fenwick

Hawman A. C.

H. Schmidt
Preston

PRINTED by
1 CDN PRINT DET, RCASC, CMHQ